The Getaway Guide to
Agatha Christie's England

The Getaway Guide to
Agatha Christie's England

Judith Diana Hurdle

RDR Books
Oakland, California

For Neil and Diane
Great travellers and boon companions

The Getaway Guide to Agatha Christie's England

RDR Books
4456 Piedmont Avenue
Oakland, California 94611

© 1999 by Judith Diana Hurdle
First Edition

ISBN 1-57143-071-7

Library of Congress Catalog Card Number: 98-067940

Book design by Paula Morrison
Cover design by Jennifer Braham
Cover photos by Robert Holmes
Edited by Bob Drews
Maps by Robert Cribley
Researcher: Julie Wulferdingen

Distributed in Canada by General Distribution Services, 325 Humber College Boulevard, Toronto, Ontario M9W 7C3

Distributed in England and Europe by Airlift Book Company, 8 The Arena, Mollison Avenue, Enfield, Middlesex EN3 7NJ England

Distributed in Australia and New Zealand by Astam Books pty Ltd 57–61 John Street Leichardt, New South Wales 2038, Australia

Printed in the United States of America

Table of Contents

supper at the Savoy. Solve the mystery of which hotel inspired her book At Bertram's Hotel. *Find revealed the intricacies of the London Gentlemen's Clubs as well as those where Christie's women congregated.*

Part II: Venturing Beyond London

Part III: The Getaway Guide

Overview

M ORE THAN TWO BILLION mystery readers world-wide have purchased Agatha Christie's books. Countless others borrow copies from libraries or friends. Her readers range in age from junior high schoolers routinely assigned *Ten Little Indians* in English class to loyal fans who re-read her mysteries again and again. Readers all over the world try to solve the crime before Miss Marple and Hercule Poirot work their magic.

Christie used a combination of imagination and recollection, creating an oddly familiar world that readers could identify even if they had never been to England. And for those lucky enough to go—well, it's almost like a trip back home. On my first trip into Christie country I took a walking holiday in Dartmoor, based at The Moorland Hotel where Agatha Christie stayed for two weeks in 1916 while completing her first book, *The Mysterious Affair at Styles*. It was there that I discovered how a place, though changed over a period of 75 years, could create an unforgettable atmosphere. The old-fashioned country hotel, the thatched-roof villages, the wind-swept moors and threatening Dartmoor prison made the sources of her inspiration apparent.

But during a trip to Torquay, her birthplace on the nearby English Riviera, and a visit to the elegant Art Deco hotel on Burgh Island that inspired *Evil Under the Sun*, I discovered one of the greatest mysteries of all. As I set off in earnest on the Agatha Christie trail, I could find no book to serve as a guide to the England the world's best-selling author knew and used in her mysteries. Though guides to individual sections of the country associated with her have appeared, no one had written a singular definitive guide to the places Agatha Christie, the world's best selling author, knew, cherished and loved.

And so that is how this work came to be. *The Getaway Guide to Agatha Christie's England* will appeal to Christie fans worldwide. Any of the 10 million tourists who come to London annually, including over 2 million Americans, will discover accessible but relatively uncrowded places to visit. Both armchair and real-life travelers will find themselves transported to lovely, little-known neighborhoods as they visit the sites of Christie's nine London residences. They will shop—as she, Poirot and Miss Marple did—at stores familiar to everyone and at stores only Londoners know. In a trip to the British Museum, they will see the Mesopotamian archaeological treasures she helped her second husband, Sir Max Mallowan, unearth in the Middle East. They will find the hotels, clubs, restaurants and tea rooms she and her characters frequented.

Using London as a base, readers will experience the glamour of a trip on the Orient Express without leaving England. They will take day trips to pursue the Christie trail farther afield. They will enjoy an outing to the elegant spa town where Christie spent the 11 days of her disappearance. On trains from Paddington Station they will visit Torquay, her hometown on the beautiful English Riviera. Burgh Island Hotel, secret hideaway for the rich and famous and inspiration for two Christie mysteries, will beckon readers to Bigbury-on-Sea. And in Wallingford, where Christie and her husband Max maintained a house for 40 years until her death in 1976, readers will become immersed in a real-life St. Mary Mead, sans the superficial prettiness.

Though the Christie connections to each of these places may inspire further exploration, each of the sites merits a visit in its own right and provides a glimpse of an England seldom seen by the ordinary tourist. Practical advice, including maps, suggested itineraries, phone numbers and other sights in the area, make planning easier. So, a Christie fan need feel no guilt even if accompanied by someone indifferent to Agatha's work: a good time will be had by all.

Agatha Christie: A Short Biography

It may surprise you to know that Agatha Christie, famous for her detective stories, also wrote a series of romance novels using the pseudonym Mary Westmacott. But Christie herself did indeed live a life as portrayed in her novels, one fraught with adventure, mystery and love.

But for chance, Agatha Mary Clarissa Miller would have been born and raised in America. Her parents—an English mother and an American father—were vacationing in Torquay, where they had married in 1878, and where their first child Margaret Frary Miller—"Madge"—was born in 1879. They had every intention of returning to America, where their second child and only son, Louis Montant—"Monty"—had been born in 1880. But business matters in New York recalled Frederick Alvah Miller to America. Not wishing to disrupt his family's holiday, he advised his wife, Clarissa Mary Boehmer—"Clara"—to find furnished lodgings to rent for a year or two. Instead, using money her father-in-law, Nathaniel Miller had left her, she bought Ashfield, a large, airy house she couldn't resist. Its location on Barton Road enhanced its appeal. Perched on a hill in Tor Mohun, the oldest section of town, it overlooked the beautiful harbor of Torbay to the south and the soft green Devonshire countryside to the north. When Frederick returned, he must have been surprised by his wife's seemingly impulsive purchase. Nevertheless, the Millers decided to make Torquay their permanent home. So their third child, Agatha, was born not in America, but in England on September 15, 1890.

Romance in an earlier generation figured in Agatha's family. Her grandmother, Mary Ann West, along with her 11 orphaned siblings, were raised by childless relatives on a farm in Sussex. In 1851, she married Frederick Boehmer of the Argyll Highlanders despite her family's reservations (she was 16 and he was 36 and they had just met). Captain Boehmer's postings took them abroad and while stationed on the Isle of Jersey, he was thrown from his horse and killed. Unfortunately, he had unwisely invested his savings, and Mary Ann found herself a nearly penniless 27-year-old widow with four children to support on a tiny pension.

In contrast, her sister, Margaret West, had fared rather well. While working at a hotel in Portsmouth, she met a wealthy American widower and they married in 1863, a few weeks before Mary Ann became a widow. Nathaniel Frary Miller could have been the hero of an Horatio Alger novel. Born a poor boy in Massachusetts, he took an office job with the milling firm of H. B. Chaflin in New York City and worked his way into a partnership, amassing a fortune along the way. When his wife, Martha—a hospital nurse—died, their only child, Frederick, grew up in the care of his grandparents in America. Nathaniel frequently came to England on business and after his marriage to Margaret, settled in Cheshire near the firm's branch in industrial Midlands Manchester.

Realizing her sister's difficult financial position, Margaret offered to rear one of Mary Ann's children, and so, at the age of 9, Agatha's mother Clara was raised by relations, as her mother before her had been. But the circumstances were very different, as Clara was not entirely an orphan and she enjoyed many advantages in the comfortable household. A momentous acquaintance resulted when she met the love of her life, her 17-year-old cousin-by-marriage, Nathaniel's son, Frederick Alvah Miller. Despite the differences in their ages and upbringing—Clara was carefully and quietly reared as befitted a young girl in the Age of Queen Victoria; Frederick went to school in Switzerland and spent his youth frolicking with the families of New York City's upper class—their romance blossomed and they married when she was 24 and he 32. Like her mother, Clara married an older man named Frederick. These were Agatha's parents.

Torquay suited the Millers. Frederick found the life congenial to his nature. He had an easy-going, affable, outgoing personality and in America had scores of friends whose names, like his (and Clara's after their marriage), appeared in the New York Social Register. Agatha's birth certificate listed his profession as "gentleman" and indeed, he fulfilled the requirements exactly: a man who did not have to work but had sufficient income to live an attractively comfortable life. Accustomed to spending days at the Union Club in New York, he very much liked the Torquay Yacht Club and his

London club, Boodles, whose membership consisted of country gentlemen like himself. Ashfield had both the space and the staff for the Millers to entertain frequently. As an avid collector he filled the rooms with bibelots purchased in Torquay's fine antique shops.

With two older siblings away at school (Madge at Roedean, Monty at Harrow), Agatha was for all practical purposes an only child. She had her parents, her devoted Nursie, her dog Tony and Ashfield to herself. Her mother decided to follow a new child-rearing trend and Agatha did not go away to school. Instead she had free run of Ashfield's expansive grounds, access to the wonderful books in its library to spark her rich imagination, and lessons taken in her own home. Clara was a magical presence in her life, regaling her with stories of her own devising. What's more, Agatha had two doting grandmothers to visit—in London's Bayswater, her birth grandmother, Mary Ann West Boehmer, called Grannie B, and in Ealing, her stepgrandmother, Margaret West Miller, called Auntie-Grannie. By all accounts—hers and others— she had a wonderfully happy childhood.

The idyll ended abruptly in 1901 when she was 11. Her father, troubled for nearly two years with heart problems, succumbed to pneumonia. Like Frederick Boehmer before him, Frederick Miller left his wife in severely reduced circumstances. Grieving over the loss of the man she truly loved and distraught with worry over money matters, Clara wanted to sell Ashfield. But her children, particularly Agatha, prevailed. Life still changed radically for Agatha. She and her mother grew even closer and more dependent upon one another. They lived quietly. Madge had married well and they spent holidays at Cheadle in Cheshire with the Watts family at Abney Hall and later with Madge and James at Manor

Hall. Agatha took full advantage of the delights Torquay offered—beaches, bathing, picnics, roller skating on the Pier. Financial difficulties did not change their social standing.

Clara made sure that Agatha enjoyed important advantages. Remembering a ploy Frederick had used when their family's austere circumstances required economies, Clara let Ashfield. She and Agatha went to the continent where living expenses were much lower. Agatha believed the two winters and one summer she spent in Paris were some of the happiest days of her life. Her mother had come armed with letters of introduction to interesting people who showed them an active social and cultural life. Agatha attended finishing school and very much enjoyed her piano lessons, though not the performances.

When they returned to Torquay, it was time for Agatha's coming out, a necessity for a girl of her class. A season in London or one in New York like Madge's was out of the question. But Clara, using her need for a warmer climate as an excuse, found an affordable locale. So in 1907, Agatha Christie had her season in Cairo. She had a wonderful time among the military and civil servants who administered the Empire in Egypt. She had an exciting and satisfying introduction to the exotic Middle East though she paid no attention to archaeology on this trip.

Back in Torquay, the romance continued, fulfilling a young girl's dreams of finding her love. She found her three most ardent suitors wanting—Byron Fletcher, Wilfred Pirie and Reggie Lucy. Then, like her Grannie B, she was swept off her feet by a good-looking officer. Lt. Archibald Christie, stationed in Exeter with the Royal Field Artillery, awaited acceptance into the just-formed Royal Flying Corps. On January 2, 1912, Agatha Miller and Archie Christie danced the night away at Lord and Lady Clifford's ball at Ugbrooke House near Chudleigh. When he drove up to Ashfield a few days later on his motor bike, claiming he was just passing by, they began their courtship. Not surprisingly, Clara insisted they wait to marry until Archie could earn enough to support them. For a year and a half they endured enforced separations as Archie's preparation took him away from Devonshire into increasingly dangerous training. With the guns of August 1914, the danger peaked. The Royal Flying Corps mobilized immediately. On August 12, Archie sailed from Southampton for France where he saw immediate action, distinguishing himself in battle and surviving the carnage of the Marne and Aisne.

Meanwhile, Agatha saw her share of pain and death. She became a Voluntary Aid Detachment practical nurse at the Red Cross Hospital in Torquay where the physical and psychological casualties came to be repaired and sent again into battle. When Archie took his first leave, on December 21, their relationship resumed its former pattern, with one seeking marriage and the other refusing. Finally, after turning each other down several times, Archie won Agatha's hand and the couple were married by special arrangement on December 24 in Clifton. His stepfather and a passerby served as witnesses. The newlyweds left immediately for Torquay, arriving after a horrendous train journey to spend Christmas Day with Madge and Clara. Boxing Day involved another train journey as Agatha saw Archie off in London, beginning a six-month separation.

In 1916 two important things happened: Agatha took a Voluntary Aid Detachment assignment in the Dispensary at Castle Chambers, where she acquired her knowledge of poisons and began studying for the Society of Apothecaries examination which she passed in 1918; with time on her hands, she began writing detective fiction, completing her first novel during a two-week stay at the Moorland Hotel on Dartmoor. She was influenced in her choice of genre by several factors— the increasing popularity of crime fiction, her mother's interest in the paranormal, Madge's publication success and her sister's challenge to write a detective story. Two publishers refused *The Mysterious Affair at Styles* and when the third, The Bodley Head, never returned her manuscript, she forgot about it. Events in her life took precedence.

When Archie took a posting as a colonel at the Air Ministry in the last months of the war, Agatha joined him in London and they set up housekeeping at 5 Northwick Terrace. After the war, Archie took an entry level job in the City. Agatha became pregnant and on August 5, 1919, gave birth to Rosalind at Ashfield. The Christies moved into a larger apartment and John Lane of The Bodley Head decided to publish Agatha's novel. It appeared in 1920, followed two years later by a thriller, *The Secret Adversary*.

In 1922, the Christies took a great risk, agreeing that no such opportunity was likely to occur again. Without a guaranteed job upon their return, Agatha and Archie set off on a round-the-world tour as part of an expedition to promote a proposed exposition of the British Empire in London. Rosalind was no problem since she had a nurse, and Clara and Madge were delighted to take charge. The adventurous tour exceeded their expectations in many ways. In addition to the exotic locales and fascinating people, there was a series of comic misadventures attributable to the inefficiency of their leader, Major E. A. Belcher, Archie's acquaintance from Clifton school days. With great relief, the Christies ended the tour by themselves, surfing in Hawaii.

The marriage endured some rough patches as Archie struggled to find a suitable position. When at last he did, they purchased a house with an unhappy reputation that their own experiences reinforced. They renamed it Styles House in honor of Agatha's book. The couple chose Sunningdale, a suburb in the stockbroker belt, because it offered an easy commute into London and featured a golf course Archie played frequently. Following his lead, Agatha took up the sport and became rather good at it, even winning a trophy.

The year 1926 was dreadful for Agatha. Only the publication of her first really successful book, *The Murder of Roger Ackroyd*, saved her from total disaster. Clara, who had been ailing for some time, died while Archie was on a business trip to Spain. Agatha, grieving over the loss of her confidante and staunchest supporter, received no comfort from Archie upon his return. She spent six exhausting weeks at Ashfield, trying to get the house and her mother's affairs in order. She and Archie were also having problems of their own. In December, after moving out on several occasions, he asked Agatha for a divorce. Archie had fallen in love with Nancy Neele whom he had met on a golfing weekend.

On December 3, Agatha Christie disappeared. She abandoned her car not far from the house and 11 days later Archie identified her at the Hydropathic Hotel (now The Old Swan) in Harrogate where she had been staying under the name of Mrs. T(h)eresa Neele. Her disappearance, her means of getting to Harrogate—all are shrouded in mystery. Her doctors diagnosed an hysterical fugue and indeed, she had been disoriented for some time, clearly in a perilous mental state. The marriage was over, though Agatha hung on for a year longer, hoping that Archie would change his mind. Their divorce was final in 1928.

Slowly, she put her life back together. She sensed a new beginning when she decided to take a trip by herself for the first time. On a whim she chose to take the Orient Express to Baghdad and then to present herself at the Ur dig, armed with letters of introduction to Sir Leonard and Lady Katharine Woolley. In early 1929 she bought a tiny mews house in London at 22 Cresswell Place, proudly using the money she had earned from her book. The Woolleys stayed there in the summer. In February 1930, at the Woolleys' invitation, she made her fateful second trip to Ur. There she met Max Mallowan, Sir Leonard's assistant. His duties included escorting visitors. He took Agatha on a round of sightseeing and, when Rosalind was reported ill in England, accompanied her on the journey home as far as Paris. In their respective memoirs *(An Autobiography* and *Mallowan's Memoirs)*, Agatha and Max give romantic accounts of their meeting, courtship, marriage in Edinburgh on September 11, and honeymoon. Agatha's only hesitancy concerned age—she was 14 years older than he—but in all other respects they were a match. Their marriage lasted 45 years until Agatha's death in 1976.

Before the war interrupted their expeditions, the adventure continued. Agatha accompanied Max every year, helping with the work on the dig and continuing to write detective fiction, by now best sellers. She could write anywhere: all she needed was a flat surface on which to set up her trusty Remington typewriter. Her account of life on a dig, *Come, Tell Me How You Live*, makes delightful reading. Max made important discoveries and proudly pointed out items in the British Museum that Agatha had a hand in uncovering.

In 1934, they bought a large, comfortable country house in Wallingford. Agatha liked Winterbrook House very much but always called it Max's house—it was an easy train ride to both London and Oxford for his work in both places. In 1938, at Max's suggestion she sold Ashfield (a secondary school and a psychiatric institution now spoiled its former views) and bought Greenway House on the River Dart between Torquay and Dartmouth, a property her mother had admired for its Georgian elegance. The Mallowans divided their time between various addresses in London and their two houses until the war, when the Admiralty requisitioned Greenway House because of its strategic position, eventually turning it over to the United States Navy.

With World War II, life had changed again. This time, England was invaded. The bombing began on the south coast of Devon. Agatha took a refresher course in the dispensary at the Torquay hospital and joined Max in London where he worked with the Turkish Relief, then the Air Ministry in London. She also volunteered in the dispensary at University College Hospital. Together they endured the London Blitz. Later she endured it alone when Max went off to serve in the Middle East and Egypt where his Arabic made him a great asset.

There was some happiness, however. Like her mother, Rosalind married during wartime—an officer in the Royal Welsh Fusiliers, Hubert Prichard. In 1943, much to everyone's joy, their son, Mathew Prichard, was born in a Cheshire nursing home near where Madge and James Watts had inherited Abney Hall. After a short rest in London, Rosalind took Mathew to the safety of Hubert's family home in Wales. Then the worst nightmare of every soldier's wife came true. Agatha was with Rosalind in Pllywrach when the telegram arrived announcing that Hubert had been killed in action. Agatha could only lament that she could do nothing to save her daughter from suffering so much sadness.

In addition to her work with the dispensary, abortive attempts at propaganda (Graham Greene's inappropriate suggestion), and photographic intelligence work, Agatha wrote a mystery a year, some of them her best. She also wrote the one book she says satisfied her completely, one of her Mary Westmacott romance novels, *Absent in Spring*. Today, that book and her next, the nostalgic *Come, Tell Me How You Live*, make an interesting juxtaposition.

After the war Max resumed his archaeological work in the Middle East, this time at Nimrud, where Agatha began her autobiography in 1950. In 1952 *The Mousetrap* opened. Agatha had a habit of giving the rights to various family members. Her grandson Mathew still collects royalties from the longest-running play in history. The girl who had little formal schooling received an Honorary Doctor of Letters from Exeter University in her home county. Max was knighted in 1968 and Agatha declared a Dame in 1971. She lived to age 85, dying on January 12, 1976, with Max at her side. He died a year and a half later and they share the same gravestone in St. Mary's churchyard at Cholsey near Wallingford.

Any recounting of Agatha Christie's life provides only limited insight into the person behind the famous writer. Ironically, this most prolific writer—whose works have been translated into virtually every written language—managed to keep herself to herself. She wrote about dastardly deeds committed by very unhappy people, yet by all accounts she had a happy childhood and a content and satisfying life. She wrote the most famous murder mysteries in the world yet she herself was not the least bit cruel or violent. She shunned the spotlight but she was the subject of one of the largest media events of the time and continued to be pursued by the curious all her life. Though probably the most widely read writer in the world after Shakespeare, she disparaged her own talent, calling herself a sausage machine: She put the bits in, ground them up and the product emerged. Indeed, taken alone, her books reveal little except that she had a lively imagination. But that talent, combined with her romantic, adventurous, very full life, make Agatha Christie a subject of endless fascination around the world.

Chronology

1890   September 15, Agatha Mary Clarissa Miller born in Torquay.

1901   Her father, Frederick Alvah Miller, dies.

1907   Agatha's "coming out" season in Cairo.

1914   Christmas Eve, marriage in Clifton near Bristol to Archibald Christie, an officer in the Royal Flying Corps; honeymoon at the Grand Hotel, Torquay; Archie leaves for a six-month stint at the front.

1914   Agatha joins the Voluntary Aid Detachment, working as a nurse at the Red Cross Hospital in Torquay Town Hall.

1916   Spends two weeks at the Moorland Hotel, Dartmoor, to complete her first novel.

Works in the dispensary at Castle Chambers until September 1918 and passes the examination of the Society of Apothecaries, acquiring her extensive knowledge of poisons.

1918   The Christies move to London during the last months of World War I.

1919 August 5, her only child, Rosalind, born at Ashfield in Torquay.

1920 Publication of first book, *The Mysterious Affair at Styles.*

1926 Mother, Clarissa (Clara) Boehmer Miller, dies.

Archie announces that he wants a divorce.

Agatha disappears on December 3 and is discovered 11 days later in the Yorkshire spa town of Harrogate.

Publication of her first successful book, *The Murder of Roger Ackroyd.*

1928 The Christies divorce in April. Agatha takes her first trip to the Middle East, visiting archaeologist Sir Leonard Woolley and his wife, Katharine, on a dig at Ur.

1929 Agatha buys the mews house at 22 Cresswell Place, Chelsea, London, with money earned by her writing.

1930 Agatha meets Max Mallowan, Sir Leonard's assistant, on her second trip to Ur; he accompanies her as far as Paris on the return when Rosalind becomes ill at home in England.

September 11, she marries Max, 14 years her junior, in Edinburgh.

1938 Agatha and Max make their last expedition to the Middle East for the duration of World War II. Agatha purchases Greenway House on the River Dart near Torquay for a summer home.

1940 Rosalind marries Hubert Prichard, an officer in the Royal Welsh Fusiliers.

1943 Agatha's only grandchild, Mathew Prichard, born.

1944 Hubert Prichard is killed in action.

1949 Rosalind marries Anthony Hicks.

1950 Agatha begins *An Autobiography* on a dig at Nimrud.

1952 *The Mousetrap*, the world's longest running play, opens at The Ambassadors Theatre, London; Agatha gives the rights to grandson, Mathew.

1956 Agatha made Commander of the British Empire.

1961 Agatha receives an Honorary Doctorate of Letters, Exeter University.

1968 Max Mallowan knighted.

1971 Agatha made Dame of the British Empire.

1976 Agatha Christie dies, age 85, at Wallingford, Oxfordshire, January 12; buried at St. Mary's Church, in nearby Cholsey.

1978 Sir Max Mallowan dies in August at Wallingford; he and Agatha share the tombstone in St. Mary's churchyard.

A Short List: The Woman and the Writer

Memoirs

Christie, Agatha. *An Autobiography*. 1977. Charming to read and indispensable; begun in the 1950s, completed in 1965, and published a year after her death, it affords a wonderful glimpse into a lost era as well as into her life and art.

Mallowan, Agatha Christie. *Come, Tell Me How You Live*. 1946. Though ostensibly an account of life on a dig with her archaeologist husband, it reveals a good deal about her.

Mallowan, Max. *Mallowan's Memoirs*. 1977. Her second husband, to whom she was married for 45 years, has two excellent chapters on her life and her work and an epilogue on their relationship.

Biography

Morgan, Janet. *Agatha Christie*. 1984. A good read. For this, the official biography, the family allowed access to material no outsider can see even today.

Studies of Her Life and Work

Barnard, Robert. *A Talent to Deceive: An Appreciation of Agatha Christie*. 1980. Reissued 1987, 1990. The author, a fine mystery writer in his own right, refutes the criticisms of her work and then offers an analysis that helps explain her continuing popularity.

Gill, Gillian. *Agatha Christie: The Woman and Her Mysteries*. 1990. A very readable, well-researched scholarly look at the woman behind the work; interesting speculation on how her life explains her work, much of which has become accepted theory.

Sova, Dawn B. *Agatha Christie A to Z: The Essential Reference to Her Life and Writings*. With an Introduction by Mathew Prichard, Christie's grandson and chairman of Agatha Christie Ltd. 1996. A terrific guide to every work, character, film and major event in her life.

Choice Christies

When she was writing *An Autobiography* in the 1960s, Agatha Christie found that two of her detective books—*The Crooked House* and *Ordeal by Innocence*—still satisfied her. Curiously, neither features Miss Marple nor Hercule Poirot.

But she was surprised to discover that, upon re-reading the others, she found one featuring Miss Marple that did please her—*The Moving Finger*. Her favorite collection of short stories featured a character she never used in a longer work: The *Mysterious Mr. Quin*.

Christie's husband, Max Mallowan, reported in his memoirs that she had two more favorites: The *Murder of Roger Ackroyd*, a Poirot mystery, and *The Pale Horse* with Agatha's alter-ego, Mrs. Oliver. He had his own addition to her list, *Endless Night*.

Humbly, here is my own list of 14:

The ABC Murders/The Alphabet Murders but avoid the absolutely unwatchable film with Tony Randall and Robert Morse!

Cards on the Table
Cat Among the Pigeons
Five Little Pigs/Murder in Retrospect
4:50 from Paddington/What Mrs. McGillicuddy Saw
Hercule Poirot's Christmas/Murder for Christmas
The Hollow
A Murder Is Announced
Murder Is Easy/Easy to Kill
The Mysterious Affair at Styles
The Pale Horse
The Sittaford Mystery/Murder at Hazelmoor
Taken at the Flood/There Is a Tide
Towards Zero

Agatha Christie's London

1

London Residences

Agatha Christie's fascination with houses defined her character. She was at her happiest looking at them, owning them, exchanging them, furnishing them, decorating them and re-doing them. At one time before the outbreak of the Second World War, she owned eight. "Houses! God bless Houses!" she exclaimed in her autobiography.

Visiting the sites of the flats and houses she occupied over the years, you will discover lovely residential neighborhoods unknown to most visitors and understand why London has been called a collection of small villages.

St. John's Wood: Before World War I, many artists lived in St. John's Wood, which then consisted almost entirely of detached and semi-detached private houses with large gardens. When Agatha and Archie Christie first moved to London in 1918 during the last months of the war, they lived at **5 Northwick Terrace,** in one of the district's big, old-fashioned houses. They chose a rather shabbily furnished two-bedroom flat instead of a larger one available elsewhere partly because Agatha felt drawn to Mrs. Woods who offered to "do" for them. That jolly, cozy woman taught Agatha the ins and outs of wartime housekeeping; her presence compensated for the inconvenience of the tiny kitchen and the beds "full of large, iron lumps."

Though a '50s-style semi-detached house now occupies the site at Number 5, several buildings like the Christies' rental still stand on Northwick Terrace. The block-long street, located off Maida Vale Road a few blocks south of Lord's Cricket Ground, ends at Aberdeen Place. There the Canal Footpath comes up to street level, before it returns to water level following Regent's Canal as it winds behind Regent's Park and leads to Primrose Hill. For refreshment before, during or after, walkers can call at a splendid Victorian Pub—Crockers Folly—on Aberdeen Place. Alternatively, those in search of a less strenuous journey can opt for lunch aboard one of the picturesque Canal Waterbuses for hire at the Little Venice landing stage, mid-way between the Tube station and Northwick Terrace. Passengers lounge in comfort as they drift past colorful terraced Georgian houses, gorgeous mansions overlooking lovely gardens and the London Zoo. They can disembark at Camden Town for the teeming outdoor markets or stay on board for the return journey to Little Venice.

Tube: Warwick Ave.

West Kensington: In 1919, one year after the end of World War I and with housing in very short supply, Agatha and Archie Christie managed to find a furnished ground floor flat in a building block behind Olympia Exhibition Centre. **25 Addison Mansions** was just large enough to accommodate them, along with the infant Rosalind, her nurse Jessie Swannell and Lucy, their cook and maid from Devonshire days who fortunately had returned from service in the WAAF.

But they soon moved to a more agreeable accommodation across the courtyard at **96 Addison Mansions**. Agatha set about redecorating the four bedrooms and two sitting rooms of the wonderful, airy flat. They lived there happily until 1922, when Agatha and Archie went on a year-long round-the-world business trip.

Agatha had one complaint—the distance from Addison Mansions to Holland Park. "Pushing the pram there and back was no joke." However, a visit to the park and its neighborhood reveals why they made the trek, aside from Rosalind's need for an outing. At 12 Holland Park Road, they would pass the delightfully eccentric Leighton House Art Gallery and Museum, with decor and works by artists of the Victorian High Renaissance. Fine Victorian houses and a number of embassies surround Holland Park. Its mixture of exotic and indigenous plants and animals, its statues, idiosyncratic buildings, Rose, Dutch and Iris gardens and the art exhibitions and concerts held there make it one of London's most delightful retreats. Holland Park residents Harold Pinter, the playwright, and Baroness P. D. James, the mystery novelist, can attest to that.

Addison Mansions no longer exists: J. Lyons & Co., a catering firm that threatened to tear down the two building blocks for expansion during the Christies' sojourn, finally did so 30 years later to build its headquarters, Cadby Hall. The exhibition center, Olympia, has had several additions since the early '20s and continues to be used for every imaginable kind of show, ranging from automobile to horse to music. Exhibition-goers add to the traffic that now whizzes along Hammersmith Road as it becomes Kensington High Street leading into central London.

Tube: Olympia/Kensington.

Chelsea: Agatha Christie owned two Chelsea residences, neither of which she sold in her lifetime. She purchased one in 1929 when she was the newly divorced famous author. She acquired the other in 1948 when she was Agatha Christie Mallowan, by then an even more famous author and the wife of a noted archaeologist.

Chelsea has attracted famous residents since the 1700s. Though originally a fishing village, in the 16th century it became home to courtiers such as Sir Thomas More. In the 17th century, the construction of the Royal Hospital for retired soldiers enlarged its population, but for a hundred years it was considered a sort of backwater. Then, in the 19th century, artists, writers and intellectuals came for its peaceful, quiet parks and the charm of its mellow red brick houses. Artistic celebrities—painters Dante Gabriel Rossetti and James McNeill Whistler, and writers George Eliot, Oscar Wilde and Henry James—gave it a reputation as a Bohemia, but intellectuals—Thomas Carlyle and the designer of bridges and tunnels, Sir Marc Brunel, father of the great engineer, Isambard Kingdom Brunel—lent it credibility.

In the 1950s, the original "Angry Young Man," John Osborne, and other iconoclastic dramatists moved to Chelsea, using their influence to make it fashionable again. Rock musicians, led by the Rolling Stones, gave it *cachet* in the '60s. Other notables have lived in the district, from philosopher Bertrand Russell and writer-director-actor Peter Ustinov (Poirot in *Evil under the Sun* and *Death on the Nile*) to such disparate denizens as J. Paul Getty Jr. and Margaret Thatcher. Blue ceramic plaques mark many buildings, recording the names and occupancy dates of celebrities. Such a plaque marks **22 Cresswell Place**, which Christie bought in 1929.

After her divorce from Archie and a trip to the Canary

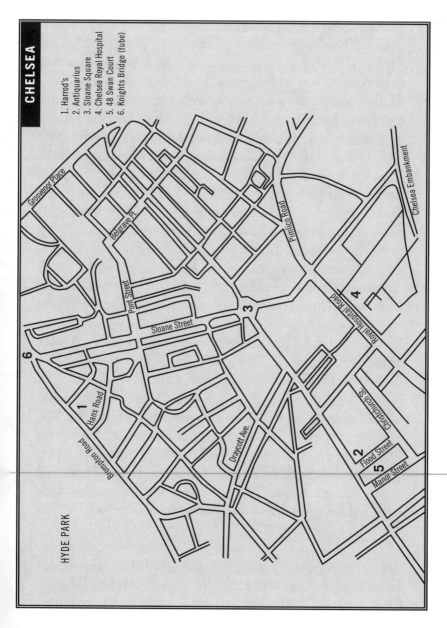

CHELSEA

1. Harrod's
2. Antiquarius
3. Sloane Square
4. Chelsea Royal Hospital
5. 48 Swan Court
6. Knights Bridge (tube)

HYDE PARK

Grosvenor Place
Belgrave Pl.
Pont Street
Sloane Street
Pimlico Road
Royal Hospital Road
Chelsea Embankment
Hans Road
Brompton Road
Draycott Ave.
Christchurch St.
Flood Street
Manor Street

Islands, Agatha purchased 22 Cresswell Place with proceeds from her books. She never sold this house and she may have felt particularly attached to it because she alone had earned the money to buy it. The small, narrow mews house underwent significant renovation to accommodate Rosalind, Agatha and Carlo, her secretary. The rearrangements created a garage, large room and maid's room downstairs; and upstairs, two bedrooms (one doubling as a dining room), a handsome bathroom done up in green, and a minuscule kitchen in which Agatha miraculously produced memorable meals. The stairs were dark and narrow, damp seeped in, and one of the windows looked out on a blank wall. These disadvantages may explain why, through the years, she moved in and out, letting and lending the place frequently. During her first year of ownership, she made a lucky loan, to Sir Leonard and Lady Woolley, the couple who later introduced her to a young archaeologist when she accompanied them on one of Sir Leonard's digs in Ur, Mesopotamia. Agatha married Max Mallowan in 1930, less than a year after that meeting.

Agatha Christie's house in its peaceful mews proves that, beneath its Bohemian veneer, Chelsea remains quietly sedate and respectable, a delightful village within a busy city. For example, behind Cresswell Place, just off the Old Brompton Road, lies The Boltons, an oval enclosure formed by two crescents with St. Mary's Church in the center; and clustered around the green space, pleasant semi-detached houses with large gardens make up a peaceful residential area.

Tube: Gloucester Road or Sloane Square.

The other Agatha Christie residence in Chelsea is quite different from 22 Cresswell Place. In 1948, the Mallowans took a flat just south of the King's Road at **48 Swan Court**, where

Agatha worked on *Witness for the Prosecution* and *The Crooked House*. The building's restaurant served the rich food she so enjoyed, and she could dine there with such friends as her next-door neighbor, Dame Sybil Thorndike. The immense apartment block, dating from the '30s, extends from Flood Street to Manor Street and remains a highly sought-after address. A maze of charming little residential streets such as Oakley and Old Church run near Swan Court. Elegant Georgian town houses, many with blue plaques, line nearby Cheyne Walk facing the river. Agatha memorialized Chelsea in *One, Two, Buckle My Shoe/The Patriotic Murders;* Alistair Blunt, the powerful financial wizard, lives in elegant simplicity in the fictional Gothic House along Chelsea Embankment

Just a block over from Swan Court, King's Road, a private roadway until 1830, bustles with life. Its eastern boundary, Sloane Square, is an area frequented by Sloane's Rangers, a group of the particularly affluent young. It was a favorite of Diana Spencer. King's Road serves as Chelsea's High Street, crowded with boutiques, traditional British pubs and fine department stores. The Chelsea Antiques Fair draws collectors to the Town Hall in September and March, but customers flock year round to the Antiquarius Center at 131–141, an antiques arcade at 181 and the Chelsea Antique Market at 245–53.

Despite the bustle, the village atmosphere persists. Most of the pedestrians live in Chelsea, from the children trundled along in push chairs to the Chelsea pensioners sitting on the benches lining the street. The retired British servicemen proudly wear their distinctive 18th century uniforms, blue in winter, red in summer. They live in the nearby Royal Hospital, whose Great Hall, chapel and gardens—the site of the

Chelsea Flower Show in May—are open to the public. A visit to Chelsea helps explain why Christie lived there longer than in any other part of London.

Tube: Sloane Square.

Campden Hill: Situated on the north side of Kensington High Street, between Holland Park and Kensington Palace, the district of Campden Hill is one of the most agreeable residential quarters in London. Built on ground 130 feet above the Thames, it contains many old world mansions formerly tenanted by people of such exalted rank that the district was nicknamed "the Dukeries." The mansions and other large houses stand in extensive park-like grounds. Despite some modernization, the district retains its rural quality. Walled lanes run between the various houses and mile-long Holland Walk skirts the east side of Holland Park, passing over the top of Campden Hill; either route allows you to enjoy a pleasant ramble, away from the din of traffic.

In 1930 Agatha and Max Mallowan acquired a house encompassing **47 and 48 Campden Street**, between Campden Hill Road and Kensington Church Street. The location was particularly appealing because Max could take the tube from Nottinghill Gate to the Tottenham Court Road stop for his archaelogical work at the British Museum. Though Agatha said the house didn't feel really right, the Mallowans kept it well into World War II, probably because of its location on a quiet street. When they sold that house, it brought a very good price because Christie's secretary Carlo, incensed by the prospective buyers' rude comments, upped the price five hundred pounds. Even now the beautifully maintained property would fetch top price.

Finally, in 1934, Agatha Christie had, for the first and last time, a room of her own in which to work. **48 Sheffield Terrace**, just two blocks below Campden Street, was *the* place she claimed she wanted to live as badly as she had ever wanted to live anywhere. The rooms, though not many, were large. She and Max each had a study. He housed his library, spread out his papers and pottery, and even designed a flawlessly functioning chimney. Her workplace had a piano, a large firm table, a hard upright typing chair, a divan, an easy chair and, most important for her, no telephone. In *An Autobiography*, Agatha lovingly describes the privacy, "the feeling of space round you—of being able to deploy yourself," that only a truly large room gives. She even had the satisfaction of solving an actual mystery there. No one but she could smell the gas that permeated their bedroom. She said she drove nearly everyone insane—builders, gas people, plumbers, her family—until she was vindicated by the discovery of an obsolete gas main under the house. "I was so conceited about having been proved right on this point that I was unbearable to live with for some time," she gloated.

Sadly, the Mallowans were forced to vacate the "perfect" house. During World War II, Agatha and Max had come up to London from Greenway House in Devon and lived at Sheffield Terrace once their renters had moved out. During the October 1944 bombing raids, when they were away for the weekend, a landmine exploded across the street, destroying three houses. It blew up their basement (which Agatha had always disliked), the roof and top floor. Even if they had been at home, they would have survived: Agatha never went into bomb shelters, fearing entrapment underground, and she and Max always slept in their bedroom on the first floor (American second floor). But she turned the near tragedy to good use: *Taken at the Flood* opens with an account of the episode at Sheffield Terrace with the addition of a body in the blown-out basement. In true Christie fashion, nothing is as it seems in the novel: death did not result from the bomb; murder is afoot.

Today, a handsome block of flats occupies the bombed site diagonally across from 48 Sheffield Terrace. The damaged buildings have been sympathetically restored. Only a roof different from that of its neighbors attests to the damage to the Mallowan house. The street has retained its village character. Pedestrians greet passersby. Roses spill over fences. A lovingly maintained Georgian post box has pride of place in the center of a walkway. Truly, a stroll up Campden Hill feels like a walk on a country road.

Tube: Nottinghill Gate or, the more picturesque route, Holland Park.

Mayfair/St. James: During World War II, when Agatha decided to join Max in London where he was working with the Turkish Relief, Sheffield Terrace had tenants. As a result, he found a flat in **Half Moon Street**. Though they lived there only a week, Agatha never forgot it due to its nasty condition. "It stood up like a tooth" as the only house left standing after the early air raids had played havoc with the buildings on the north side of Piccadilly. Despite its location in London's poshest section directly across from Green Park and the Ritz, it smelled horribly of dirt, grease and cheap scent.

Next, they lived in **Park Place**, conveniently located just off St. James Street, around the corner from the Ritz and almost directly opposite Boodles, their club. But in war time, nothing was as it had been. The poor waiters at Boodles had to serve meals in the evening, then make their way home through the air raids. When the tenants in Sheffield Terrace asked to give up their lease, the Mallowans were not sorry to return there.

Today's visitor to Mayfair and St. James would have a hard time imagining the districts in the '40s during the Mallowans' short stay. These areas have been restored to their former splendor. Piccadilly separates the two districts. This broad avenue is lined with first-class hotels, splendid dwellings and legendary shops such as Fortnum and Mason's and Hatchard's book shop. The Burlington Arcade, supervised by "beadles" in coats and bowler hats who close the gates at night, contains 41 luxurious shops. In the Green Park Tube station, below ground at its north entrance, is a full-sized luxury automobile showroom.

North of Piccadilly, extending as far as Oxford Street, lies Mayfair, the wealthiest and most expensive part of London. Grand houses surround its numerous squares such as Berkeley, Grosvenor and Hanover; prosperous businesses, including designer shops, galleries and antique shops, line Old and New Bond Streets.

South of Piccadilly, elegant and quietly refined St. James extends as far as St. James Park. It is the purview of gracious townhouses, exclusive gentlemen's clubs, and along St. James and Jermyn Streets, clothing shops and world-famous businesses that date back to the 17th century. The recently renovated St. James Club, at the end of Park Place where the Mallowans had their service flat, has opened its doors to non-members.

Tube: Green Park.

Hampstead: Agatha decided that **22 Lawn Road Flats** was a good place to be during her first separation from Max in

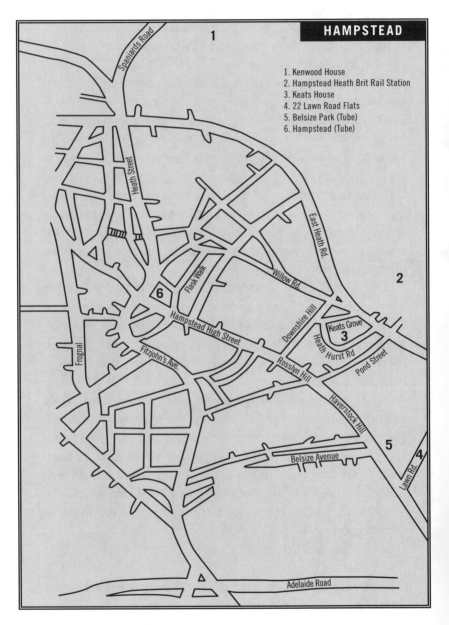

HAMPSTEAD

1. Kenwood House
2. Hampstead Heath Brit Rail Station
3. Keats House
4. 22 Lawn Road Flats
5. Belsize Park (Tube)
6. Hampstead (Tube)

10 years. He had, finally, gotten a posting to the Middle East with the Air Ministry, where he could use his Arabic in the war effort. The bombing at Sheffield Terrace had left them with no access to that flat. With their furniture stored in the new squash court at Winterbrook in Wallingford, they had moved into the block of Bauhaus flats on Lawn Road, Hampstead. Agatha started work in the dispensary at University College Hospital on Gower Street in Bloomsbury, and she could take the Northern Line five stops from Belsize Park to Warren Street.

Everything about the building pleased her. She found the people kindly, the small restaurant informal and happy, and a garden ideal for outdoor summer meals. Best of all, a bank of trees and shrubs ran behind the flats. A pyramid-shaped, double white cherry tree opposite her window cheered her every spring morning. The Mallowans left Lawn Road in 1946 when they made Cresswell Place their London base.

Neither Lawn Road Flats nor its immediate vicinity have fared very well in the 50 years since Christie lived there. The Bauhaus building that so pleased her has been converted to council flats; the building restaurant has become the lobby; and both the garden at the end flat and the bank of foliage behind the building are now overgrown and inaccessible. Chain-link fencing lines the public footpath leading through the nature preserve and a council estate of new semi-detached houses to Haverstock Hill. There, the expensive cars driven by those playing at the tennis club next to the tube station contrast sharply with the closed shop fronts.

But the area corresponds exactly to the description in her autobiography of a 10-minute walk along streets lined with country style cottages with neat front lawns. She took Carlo's Sealyham dog, James, to Hampstead Heath, the 420-acre grassy common where Londoners have come for outings since the 17th century. The open spaces, lakes and wooded groves make an ideal spot for picnics and walks. Parliament Hill Fields, high above the city, has impressive views. Open-air concerts are held at Kenwood House, a beautifully proportioned building with a Robert Adam-designed south facade and interior. Hampstead has excellent pubs and a high street packed with interesting shops. Writers and artists have always been attracted by the country atmosphere. John Keats wrote "Ode to a Nightingale" when he heard the bird's song while staying at the house which now bears his name and is open to the public. With so many attractions nearby, it's no wonder Agatha found Lawn Road Flats a congenial place to live.

Tube: Belsize Park.

Christie Works Mentioned in This Chapter

An Autobiography
Evil Under the Sun
Death on the Nile
"Witness for the-Prosecution" (Short Story in *Witness for the Prosecution and Other Stories)*
The Crooked House
One, Two, Buckle My Shoe/The Patriotic Murders
Taken at the Flood

Contacts and Resources for This Chapter

St. John's Wood

Lord's Cricket Ground, St. John's Wood Road, NW8. Telephone: (0171) 289-1611. *Tube:* St. John's Wood.

Crockers Folly Pub & Carvery, 24 Aberdeen Place, Maida Vale, NW8. Telephone: (0171) 286-6608. *Tube:* Warwick Ave.

Jason's Trip, across from 60 Blomfield Road, Little Venice, W9. Telephone: (0171) 286-3428. Book in advance to have tea or lunch aboard. Telephone: (0171) 286-6752. *Tube:* Warwick Ave.

West Kensington

Leighton House Art Gallery and Museum, 12 Holland Park Road, Kensington, W14. Telephone: (0171) 602-3316. Monday through Saturday 11 a.m. to 5 p.m.; closed Sunday. *Tube:* Holland Park.

Olympia National Hall, W14. Telephone: (0171) 373-8141. *Tube:* Olympia.

Chelsea

Chelsea Flower Show, Royal Hospital, Chelsea, SW3. Telephone: (0171) 821-3000. Late May. *Tube:* Sloane Square.

Antiquarius Antiques Centre, 131–141 King's Road, SW3. Telephone: (0171) 351-5353. Monday through Saturday 10 a.m. to 6 p.m. *Tube:* Sloane Square.

Chelsea Antiques Market, 245–253 King's Road, SW3. Telephone: (0171) 352-1720. Monday through Saturday 10 a.m. to 6 p.m. *Tube:* Sloane Square.

Royal Hospital, Royal Hospital Road, Chelsea, SW3.

Chapel and Museum open 10 a.m. to noon, weekdays and 2 p.m. to 4 p.m. on Sundays (April through September for museum). Sundays: Holy Communion 8:30 a.m., Matins 11 a.m. after Governor's Parade at 10:40 a.m. when Pensioners wear their scarlet summer or blue winter uniforms. *Tube:* Sloane Square.

Mayfair/St. James

Fortnum and Mason, 181 Piccadilly, W1. Telephone: (0171) 734-8040. Monday through Saturday 9:30 a.m. to 6 p.m. *Tube:* Green Park or Piccadilly Circus.

Hatchards Bookstore, 187 Piccadilly, W1. Telephone: (0171) 439-9921. *Tube:* Green Park or Piccadilly Circus.

Hampstead

Kenwood House, Hampstead Lane, Hampstead, NW3. Telephone: (0181) 348-1286. Open 10 a.m. to 6 p.m., til 4 p.m. October 1 to March 31, closed December 24–5. Saturday evening open-air concerts, early July to early September. Telephone: (0171) 413-1443. *Tube:* Highgate or Hampstead Heath.

Keats House, Keats Grove, NW3 Tel (0171) 435-2062. Monday through Friday 10 a.m. to 1 p.m. and 2 p.m. to 6 p.m., Saturday to 5 p.m.; Sunday, Easter and bank holidays 2 p.m. to 5 p.m.; April to October. Monday through Friday 1 p.m. to 5 p.m. Saturday 10 a.m. to 1 p.m. and 2 p.m. to 5 p.m., Sunday 2 p.m. to 5 p.m. Closed 3 days at Christmas, New Year's Day, Good Friday, Easter Eve and May Day. *Tube:* Belsize Park or Hampstead.

A London Chronology

1918–1919	5 Northwick Terrace	St. John's Wood
1919–1924	96 Addison Mansions	West Kensington
1929–1976	22 Cresswell Place	Chelsea
1930–1934	47–48 Campden Street	Campden Hill
1934–1940	48 Sheffield Terrace	Campden Hill
1939	Half Moon Street	Mayfair
1939	Park Place	St. James
c.1940–1946	22 Lawn Road Flats	Hampstead
1948–1976	48 Swan Court	Chelsea

2

Shopping in London

NAPOLEON CALLED ENGLAND "a nation of shopkeepers." Agatha Christie and her characters, in their own way, conform to that stereotype: They seem addicted to shopping. As prudent shoppers, they know where to find attractive, durable goods for themselves and their homes as well as how to best indulge an occasional splurge.

Army and Navy Stores: As a child, Agatha learned about shopping at the Army and Navy Stores from her grandmothers. Though there is only one, at **101–105 Victoria St.,** it is always referred to as "the Stores." Christie said that the Army and Navy Stores was the hub of the universe for Auntie-Grannie and Granny B. Miss Marple shared some of her beloved Auntie-Grannie's characteristics; not surprisingly she shops there when she stays *At Bertram's Hotel.* Miss Marple fondly recalls the strawberry ice cream served when, as a girl, she shopped with her aunt. In the short story "Sanctuary," Miss Marple, accompanied by her favorite godchild, Bunch, is thrilled to find "a prewar quality face towel" at a white sale, just as Auntie-Grannie was pleased to augment her collection with bath towels on sale at the Army and Navy Stores.

The large department store, just east of Victoria Station, opened in 1872 as a place intended for service men and their families. Long open to the general public, it has an excellent food hall and wine department, clothes of quality rather than fashion, household goods, toys, china and a coffee shop and restaurant on the top floor. Its well-founded reputation for value makes it easy to understand why Miss Marple and Agatha Christie's grannies chose it. And the comfortable '50s decor makes the shopper feel as if time has stopped.

Tube: Victoria or St. James Park.

Heals: When she and her first husband, Archie Christie, took a flat in Addison Mansions, Agatha had furniture sent from Ashfield, her family home in Torquay. Later she ordered good modern nursery furniture for daughter Rosalind and beds for them at Heals. She decorated the walls in Rosalind's room with a very expensive frieze from the shop.

Influenced by the Arts and Crafts Movement, Heals' founder, Sir Ambrose Heal, promoted quality vernacular furniture, as signified by the craftsmen's tools that decorate the spandrels on the store designed by Smith and Brewer in 1916. The original customers were members of the Bloomsbury Group, influential painters, writers and intellectuals, including Lydia Lopokova, the wife of economist John Maynard Keynes. They found Heals' style and location, at **198 Tottenham Court Road**, appealing.

When Sir Terence Conran owned Heals, he subdivided the property to make space for his brain-child, Habitat, offering knock-offs of Heals' unfussy, modern styles. For his success in making well-designed furniture affordable for so many people through the Habitat chain, Queen Elizabeth knighted him. However, true Londoners remain loyal to Heals and shop at sales for the store's famous bedding, fine teak and brass-trimmed furniture and children's furniture. One newspaper columnist recently wrote that an observer at the Heals' sale can see how working mothers spend their Saturdays. Sir Terence's designer restaurant is another reason for going.

The neighborhood holds a further attraction for today's visitor. In the 1930s, the area across Tottenham Court Road from the store became the hub of London literary life when the likes of the Welsh poet Dylan Thomas and English artists Augustus John, Francis Bacon and Lucien Freud drank at the Fitzroy Tavern. Officially called Fitzrovia, today this fashionable area near the British Telecom tower features wine bars, cafes and restaurants, as well as Pollock's Toy Museum at the corner of Scala and Goodge streets. Fitzroy Square, at the north end of Fitzrovia, is well worth seeing for its elegantly designed Robert Adam houses.

Tube: Goodge Street.

Libertys: Who would want to miss a visit to what is often called the most beautiful department store in London? In addition, the merchandise Libertys has on offer makes it irresistible, as Christie's characters well knew. When Sir Stafford Nye, in *Passenger to Frankfurt* neglects to bring gifts for his family from Malaya, he knows that if he goes round to Libertys, he'll find goods from exotic lands.

Housed in a distinctive building designed by E.T. and E. S. Hall in 1924, Libertys occupies an entire block at **210–220 Regent St.** at Great Marlborough Street north of the graceful Regency Quadrant which joins Piccadilly Circus. The half-timbering on the mock Tudor exterior is structural, not decorative, with timbers from men-of-war ships. The store's warm carved-wood interior, lovingly cared for, features linen

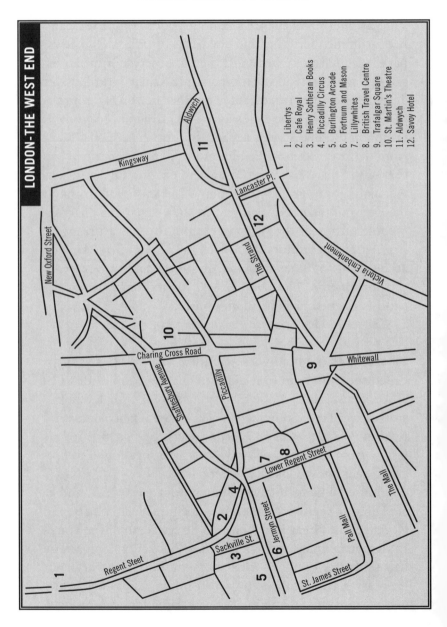

LONDON-THE WEST END

1. Libertys
2. Cafe Royal
3. Henry Sotheran Books
4. Piccadilly Circus
5. Burlington Arcade
6. Fortnum and Mason
7. Lillywhites
8. British Travel Centre
9. Trafalgar Square
10. St. Martin's Theatre
11. Aldwych
12. Savoy Hotel

fold paneling, carved balconies and plush carpets. It provides the perfect setting for display of the distinctive designs that have come to epitomize the English style. Furniture, fabrics, housewares, women's clothing and men's accessories are available in Arthur Lazenby's original Art Nouveau patterns as well as in William Morris prints. Libertys' shawls and scarves for women are especially prized. Everything in the store, from the most magnificent carpets to little handkerchiefs, has the highly sought-after Libertys look. And when the browser's energy flags after trooping from floor to floor, Libertys has a restaurant serving wonderful gooey accompaniments to a restorative cup of tea.

Tube: Oxford Circus.

Debenhams: Like Rhoda Dawes in *Cards on the Table*, the shopper approaching Debenhams risks being buffeted about by the crowds on London's longest shopping thoroughfare, Oxford Street. Rhoda mistakenly paused uncertainly on the pavement just outside the entrance before leaving to consult Christie's alter ego, Mrs. Oliver, "the chubby lady who eats apples" while she writes detective novels. The savvy shopper avoids Rhoda's fate by plunging into the huge department store at **334–338 Oxford St.**, attracted by the moderately priced fashionable merchandise that young Rhoda would have fancied. Debenhams has branches all over England, as do several of the other great department stores that extend for a mile along Oxford Street.

At **458 Oxford St.**, the largest branch of Marks and Spencers, the huge chain similar to Penney's or Sears in the United States, is the overwhelming middle class choice for excellent values in linens and clothing. In fact, one wag has observed that on any given day, upwards of 70% of the women in London are wearing knickers with the "Marks and Sparks" St. Michael label. The fresh cut sandwiches, salads and other quick foods make its foodhall very popular. The flagship John Lewis store is also on Oxford Street; always well regarded for dry goods, its partnership has acquired the upmarket grocery chain Waitrose. The most spectacular store on the street, however, is Selfridges at 400 Oxford St. It was founded in 1906 by an American, Henry Gordon Selfridge, when he could not convince his employer, Marshall Field, that Europe was ready for a full-service department store. Selfridges rivals Harrods for the variety of its offerings, though the presentation of the goods is not as spectacular. And unlike Harrods, it does not have a dress code for shoppers. A gong sounds at 3:30 to remind customers that refreshments are available in its three restaurants, four coffee shops and in a juice bar. Tea in the adjacent Selfridges Hotel makes the nicest ending to a shopping expedition along always bustling Oxford Street.

Tube: Oxford Circus, Bond Street or Marble Arch.

Lillywhites: Whether as mere pastimes or pursued in earnest, sports engage a fair number of Agatha Christie's characters, as they did Christie herself. Though some large sports equipment outfitters may offer better prices, venerable Lillywhites on **Piccadilly** near the Circus offers the widest range in London. For the traditional British sports—such as cricket, croquet, squash, bowls—it has the highest quality equipment.

Lillywhites would certainly have attracted Archie, Agatha's first husband. Because of his intense addiction to the game, they chose their house at Sunningdale for its proximity to a golf course. Early in her marriage, Agatha Christie became a good golfer, winning a trophy once she overcame her natural diffidence in competition. In two mysteries, *Murder on the Links* and *Why Didn't They Ask Evans?/the Boomerang Clue,* bodies are discovered on golf courses. However, golf lost its attraction for her when she became a "golf widow" as her marriage deteriorated and her husband left her for Nancy Neele in 1926.

Christie used her extensive knowledge of tennis in *Towards Zero,* which contains an excellent description of a match. The plot turns on the author's knowledge of the game. Lillywhites has a selection of rackets, shoes and clothing that would please even a Wimbledon participant.

Lillywhites offers an opportunity to examine beautifully finished examples of cricket bats, balls for lawn bowls and recreational as well as tournament quality croquet equipment.

Tube: Piccadilly Circus.

Whiteleys: Founded in 1863 as a butcher shop that grew into the pioneer department store on **Queensway** between Bayswater and Paddington, Whiteleys figured in a game young Agatha loved to play with Auntie-Grannie in her Ealing kitchen. In "a chicken from Mr. Whiteleys," she pretended to be the chicken ready for carving, lying so still, until the last moment when she came alive to scream, "It's Me!" Despite this happy memory, Whiteleys has association with a traumatic time in her life. At the beginning of her infamous 11-day disappearance, having abandoned her car in Surrey along with her fur coat and bag, she purchased a coat, small case and night things at Whiteleys. These tided her over until she could buy clothing in Harrogate with the several hundred pounds that, according to her secretary, she had secreted in a belt, following Auntie-Grannie's advice to keep cash handy.

The Whiteleys original building in Queensway, crowned in the center by a large dome, underwent a renovation after having been closed for many years. Now an enclosed Edwardian galleria, anchored by a Marks and Spencer, it houses some British trademark stores, as well as international chain stores, a cinema and a top tier with cafes, bars and restaurants.

Tube: Bayswater.

Asprey: The search for the perfect gift might end at the ultimate gift shop, Asprey located at **161–169 New Bond St.** on the corner of Grafton Street in elegant Mayfair. The display windows are filled with a sampling of the furniture, leather goods, silverware, jewelry and china on offer inside. Asprey has *objets d'art* to rival those at Tiffany's in New York or Gump's in San Francisco.

At Asprey, Mrs. Packington, in the short story, "The Case of the Middle-Aged Wife," bought her toy boy, Claude, a gold cigarette case. Any of Christie's beloved dogs would have been happy with the ultimate doggy treat, a French canine hamper, whose fittings include a waterproof blanket to protect delicate bones from damp or chilly grass, a stainless steel bowl, a thermos for cool water and a brush to shine up the coat. Asprey offers a satisfying selection of elegant gifts for presentation to the most discriminating recipients.

Tube: Piccadilly Circus or Green Park.

Henry Sotheran Ltd.: Agatha Christie was a voracious reader all her life. Sotheran, one of Europe's oldest antiquarian booksellers at **2 Sackville St.**, has a wonderful selection of the authors Christie loved and referred to in her novels. In her autobiography she recalls with fondness the children's adventure stories that were her first inspiration. Sotheran has recently opened a strong children's books section. Along with familiar works, such as *The Railway Children* by Edith Nesbit, which Christie mentions in *The ABC Murders,* the browser will find many of the 80 titles by one of her early favorites, G. A. Henty. The heroes in Henty's books were brave, moral and manly; at the end they always saved the lives of their future brides—just the sort of thing to fire young Agatha's imagination.

Into adulthood Christie loved adventure tales, especially Alexander Dumas' and Sir Walter Scott's. She frequently reread the great Victorians, William Makepeace Thackeray and Charles Dickens. These authors' works are Sotheran's mainstay. Because Dickens was a regular customer, Sotheran sold his library when he died.

Though Sotheran is famous for its rare books as well as prints by such luminaries as the ornithologist John Gould, it stocks many choice works well within the reach of the ordinary reader. One need not be a regular or famous customer like politicians Denis Thatcher and Edward Heath or playwright Tom Stoppard to feel welcome. For over 230 years, the shop has had—as a priority—a policy of open door to tourists, foreign students, all booklovers. With a little luck, today's browser could well find a fair copy of Christie's favorite Dickens' novel, *Bleak House.*

Tube: Piccadilly Circus.

Charbonnel et Walker: A suitable finale for any shopping spree could well end as Poirot would end his—with chocolates. Because of its truffles, Prestat at 14 Princes Arcade is said to have the best chocolate in London. However, Charbonnel et Walker is probably more Poirot's style. In an exquisite bow-fronted shop at **28 Old Bond St.** very near Asprey, the staff packs into cunning containers what many claim are the best chocolates in the world. To restore energy after such arduous shopping, it might be wise to ask for one or two of Prince Philip's favorite, a mocha baton, in a separate box.

Tube: Bond Street or Green Park.

Works Mentioned in This Chapter

An Autobiography
At Bertram's Hotel
Passenger to Frankfort
Cards on the Table
Murder on the Links
Why Didn't They Ask Evans?/The Boomerang Clue
Towards Zero
"The Case of the Middle-Aged Wife" in *Parker Pyne Investigates/Mr. Parker Pyne, Detective*
The ABC Murders

Contacts and Resources for This Chapter

General Shopping Hours in London: Monday through Saturday 9 or 10 a.m. to 5:30 or 6 p.m.; some shops open for late shopping Wednesday or Thursday until 8 p.m.

Army and Navy Stores, 101–105 Victoria St. Telephone: (0171) 834-1234. *Tube:* Victoria.

Heals, 198 Tottenham Court Rd. Telephone: (0171) 636-1666. *Tube:* Goodge St.

Pollock's Toy Museum, 41 Whitfield St. Telephone: (0171) 636-3452. *Tube:* Goodge St.

Libertys, 210–220 Regent St. Telephone: (0171) 734-1234.

Monday, Tuesday, Friday, Saturday 9:30 a.m. to 6 p.m.; Wednesday 10 a.m. to 6 p.m.; Thursday 9:30 a.m. to 7:30 p.m. *Tube:* Oxford Circus.

Debenhams, 334 Oxford St. Telephone: (0171) 580-3000. Monday, Tuesday 9:30 a.m. to 7 p.m.; Wednesday 10 a.m. to 8 p.m.; Thursday, Friday 9:30 a.m. to 8: p.m.; Saturday 9 a.m. to 7 p.m. *Tube:* Oxford Circus.

Marks and Spencer, 458 Oxford St. Telephone: (0171) 935-7954. Monday through Wednesday, and Saturday 9 a.m. to 7 p.m.; Thursday and Friday 9 a.m. to 8 p.m. *Tube:* Marble Arch.

Selfridges, 400 Oxford St. Telephone: (0171) 629-1234. Monday through Wednesday, Friday and Saturday 9:30 a.m. to 7 p.m.; Thursday 9:30 a.m. to 8 p.m.; Sunday 9:30 a.m. to 6 p.m. *Tube:* Bond St. or Marble Arch.

Lillywhites Ltd. 24–36 Lower Regent St., Piccadilly. Telephone: (0171) 915-4000. Monday, Wednesday, Friday 9:30 a.m. to 5:30 p.m.; Thursday 9:30 a.m. to 7 p.m.; Saturday 9:30 a.m. to 6 p.m. *Tube:* Piccadilly Circus.

Whiteley of Bayswater, Queensway. Telephone: (0171) 229-8844. Monday through Saturday 10 a.m. to 8 p.m.; Sunday noon to 6 p.m. *Tube:* Bayswater or Queensway.

Asprey, 161–169 New Bond St. Telephone: (0171) 493-6767. Monday through Friday 9 a.m. to 5:30 p.m.; Saturday 10 a.m. to 5 p.m. *Tube:* Green Park or Piccadilly Circus.

Henry Sotheran Ltd., 2 Sackville St., Piccadilly. Telephone: (0171) 439-5151. Monday through Friday 10 a.m. to 6 p.m.; Saturday 10 a.m. to 1 p.m. *Tube:* Piccadilly Circus.

Prestat, 14 Princes Arcade, Piccadilly. Telephone: (0171) 629-4838. Monday through Saturday 9:30 a.m. to 5:30 p.m. *Tube:* Piccadilly Circus.

Charbonnel et Walker (in the Burlington Arcade), 1 Royal Arcade, 28 Old Bond St. Telephone: (0171) 491-0939. Monday through Friday 9:30 a.m. to 5 p.m. Saturday 10 a.m. to 5 p.m. *Tube:* Bond St. or Green Park.

Burlington Arcade, Piccadilly, adjacent to the Royal Academy of Art. Telephone: (0171) 493-1764. Monday through Saturday 9 a.m. to 5:30 p.m. *Tube:* Bond St., Green Park or Piccadilly Circus.

3

On the Town

CHRISTIE'S CHARACTERS ALWAYS seem to have inside knowledge of the best spots in London for the high life. Christie herself thoroughly enjoyed the delights the city offers in the way of conviviality, food and beverages (though she drank no alcohol, preferring a cup of thick Devonshire cream diluted with a little milk). Her books contain references to unidentifiable places such as a dingy restaurant in Soho or a posh London restaurant with a floor show. But she often uses actual names or thinly disguised descriptions, pointing the way for an alert reader to find a good time on the town.

The Ritz: In Agatha Christie's world, sooner or later everyone goes, not, as in *Casablanca* to Rick's, but to the Ritz. Hastings suggests that he and Poirot drink dinner there in *The ABC Murders.* Tommy and Tuppence would spend their last pence for tea at the Ritz. Calling it the "Blitz" in *The Secret of Chimneys* doesn't fool anyone; a man of Anthony Cade's stature would consider staying only at the famed Ritz for delivering the memoirs of the late Count Stylpitch of Herzoslovakia to a certain London publisher whose identity he may not reveal.

A glamorous reputation explains the renowned establishment's popularity, and its convenient location enhances its attraction. Whether a Christie character is shopping in Mayfair, reading in the London Library, stocking up on comestibles at Fortnum and Mason, seeing to bespoke shirts and boots in Jermyn Street or simply is bored at his nearby gentlemen's club, the Ritz is just steps away. Its colonnaded arcade, reminiscent of Paris' Rue de Rivoli, extends along **Piccadilly** between Green Park and Arlington Street. Pausing in its shelter before stepping inside allows a moment for anticipating the comforts within, not the least of which are the beautifully appointed bedrooms and suites in London's largest hotel.

The Ritz excels at satisfying the inner person. The elegant Palm Court provides a Pimms Cup No. 1 dressed to perfection with summer fruits, a gin and tonic with lime, a delicate chicken sandwich for lunch, London's most famous tea, and, on weekends, big bands for after-dinner dancing. The Louis XVI Restaurant, regarded as one of the most beautiful in Europe, set the standard by which Poirot judged food. In *Curtain*, when confronted at Styles House with what he calls English cooking at its worst, Poirot remarks to Hastings that it "is not, you comprehend, the Ritz." Indeed, nothing *is* quite the ultra-sophisticated, swank hotel that requires its own word to capture its character—ritzy.

Tube: Green Park.

The Savoy: Luxurious, but lively and chic, the Savoy on The Strand exudes a completely different atmosphere than the Ritz. A fitting successor to the Duke of Lancaster's Savoy Palace that occupied the site until it burned to the ground during the Peasants' Revolt in 1381, the imposing building covers nearly an acre. On its river side, it offers sweeping vistas beyond the Victoria Embankment and across the Thames. Claude Monet was inspired to paint his magnificent views of London from a terraced balcony outside his room, though his painting location was removed in 1912 to add two stories to the hotel.

Caruso sang from a gondola when the Savoy's courtyard was flooded for a party; Pavlova danced in its beautiful ballroom and Valentino in the foyer. Gershwin gave his first London performance of *Rhapsody in Blue;* Noel Coward and Maurice Chevalier performed in the cabaret; and the *thé dansant* originated at the Savoy. Even before the hotel opened in 1889, the location had musical associations: Richard D'Oyly Carte staged Gilbert and Sullivan at the Savoy Theatre; the grannies took Agatha to see their operettas there. Today, tunes played on the Savoy's famous white piano set the mood for afternoon tea in the Thames Foyer where one can eavesdrop on London's most sophisticated crowd.

In 1954, when Agatha wanted to throw a celebration party for the opening of her play *Witness for the Prosecution,* she chose the Savoy. Following her lead, Christie's publishers gave several large parties for her at the Savoy, including one in 1958 for a thousand restaurant guests when *The Mousetrap* became the longest-running production in British theater history. However, the usually reticent Agatha called that party "hell at the Savoy" because of its size, its obvious purpose—publicity—and because, after steeling herself for the ordeal and arriving early as instructed, a porter failed to recognize her and she nearly failed to get in to the gala.

Christie's characters, however, have no problem when they come to the Savoy. Rufus Van Aldin, the American millionaire in *The Mystery of the Blue Train,* stays at the Savoy so often the staff recognizes him on sight. Poirot sends Hastings there to work as secretary for a rich American in the espionage novel *The Big Four*. Christie knew that the Savoy, the first great London hotel featuring a private bathroom in each bedroom, had become the hotel of choice for Americans. It's the Savoy for the movie star Lola Brewster in *The Mirror Crack'd*. Even Miss Marple, who, unlike everyone else, does not frequent the Ritz, slips in a Savoy hotel meal on her day trips to London. Poirot and Hastings sup in the Savoy Grill after a show in *Thirteen for Dinner/Lord Edgware Dies*. Christie told an acquaintance that she had seen a man who *was* Poirot in every way lunching in the Grill. The only thing she was able to find out was that he came from Belgium. In fiction and in real life, the Savoy is very smart indeed.

Tube: Embankment or Charing Cross.

Claridges Hotel: Miss Marple puts Claridges at the top of her list when she must choose where to meet her old American school chum who had married well. Poirot and Hastings lunch there in *Thirteen for Dinner/Lord Edgware Dies*. It is thinly disguised as Harridges in "The Golden Ball." Conspiracies, both fair and foul featuring exotic eastern Europeans, evolve there in *The Secret of Chimneys* and *The Secret Adversary*.

In the mid-19th century, Mr. Claridge bought the business begun by M. Mivart, a Frenchman who had recognized the absence of sumptuous accommodation in London. In 1895, Claridge's heirs replaced the original building, and in 1930, added substantially to it. Claridges attracts royalty and flies the flags of visiting kings, princes and presidents. Claridges' tea, served in a quietly unobtrusive room, is surely one

of the most elegant in London, offering opportunity to observe dignitaries and diplomats. The ladies cloakroom, arguably the city's finest, proves that no detail is unimportant. The hotel's quiet, dignified and understated atmosphere suited the 84-year-old wheelchair-bound Agatha when she dined there to celebrate the premier of the film *Murder on the Orient Express*. Claridges on **Brook Street at Davies** in Mayfair quite appropriately is generally named London's best hotel.
Tube: Bond St.

Flemings or Brown's? In *At Bertram's Hotel,* Christie created a mystery: She gave tantalizing descriptions of everyone's idea of the quintessential London hotel—"dignified, unostentatious, and quietly expensive"—but omitted the specifics that would enable readers to identify the particular hotel serving as the model. Either of two hotels in Mayfair—Brown's or Flemings—may have been used. However, one unimpeachable authority supports Flemings as the more likely model. Before publication, Agatha changed Bertram's manager's name because it was too close to that of the real one at Flemings. Edmund Cork, Christie's agent, told Agatha that he had changed Crescent Street to Square Street to further disguise Flemings on Half Moon Street where, in 1900, Robert Fleming, a Scot, opened a small private hotel at No. 10. The hotel currently comprises **No. 7 to 12 Half Moon Street** as well as two townhouses at the rear in Clarges Street. Extensively modernized, until very recently Flemings retained enough of its character to seem a convincing model for Bertram's.

Like Bertram's, Flemings survived the worst of the early air raids of 1940, but the houses along Half Moon Street that had flanked it were decimated, along with the entire east corner at Piccadilly. Agatha recalls with a verbal shudder the temporary flat on Half Moon Street she and Max took in a dreadful house that stood up like a tooth among the rubble.

Most convincing is Flemings' physical set-up. The big entrance lounge where tea is served is directly off reception. It provides a good view of the swing doors, making it easy for elderly ladies to observe who comes in and out, as they loved to do at Bertram's. The other public rooms at Bertram's are called retreats, known to those who wanted them; that is the sense one gets at Flemings walking down thickly carpeted passages to the bar and restaurant. The ceilings are comfortingly low, the decor chintzy, the chairs old-fashioned in design—all quite inviting for a cozy little gossip with a special friend. For some time, Flemings had been a well-kept secret, offering special half-price rates on weekends to accommodate the budget-conscious or those of limited means as did the fictional Bertram's. Alas, like Bertram's, Flemings has changed. The decor, while still retaining some of that Christie charm, has been heavily modernized, the special rate abolished, and one has a hard time imagining any of "the old dears," as Colonel Luscombe so smugly called them, feeling at home there amidst the heavily promoted meeting facilities. But until very recently, Flemings would have fit the 1955 setting of the novel.

On the other hand, Charles Osborne, a respected Christie scholar, confidently proposed Brown's as the prototype. It certainly outstrips Flemings in longevity, dating back to 1837, the year Queen Victoria came to the throne. Its location at **Albemarle and Dover Streets,** farther east of Hyde Park than Flemings, can be made to fit the ambiguous locale Christie ascribes to Bertram's—on the right hand side in a quiet street that can be reached "if you turn off an unpretentious street from the Park, and turn left and right once or twice." Like

Bertram's and Flemings, Brown's emerged relatively unscathed from World War II bombing, though neighboring structures suffered. Buildings along Dover Street disappeared, most notably the Turkish Baths where Mark Twain traipsed in his bathrobe during a stay at adjacent Brown's in 1907.

The case for Brown's has some compelling features, as a visit makes clear. The staff corresponds nicely to Christie's description of Bertam's, from the doorman with perfect deportment, to the maitre d' with the courtly manners of that long-vanished species—the perfect butler—to the bellman who happily relates stories told him by his father who worked at Brown's before the war. The hospitality and service follow the tradition established by the founder, James Brown, a retired gentleman's gentleman. The hotel's richly polished wood paneling and brass, Victorian and Edwardian antiques, sumptuous carpets, cushy chintz covered armchairs and sofas recall the Golden Age in which Christie set her novels.

The staff, the setting seem perfect. But like Miss Marple at Bertram's, the astute observer senses that something is not quite right. Where are those who Christie said "patronized [Bertram's] over a long stretch of years." One searches in vain for any sign of "the higher echelons of clergy, dowager ladies of the aristocracy up from the country, girls on their way home for the holidays from expensive finishing schools." The stage prop English to whom Mr. Humfries, Bertram's owner, gave special rates are nowhere to be seen at Brown's, probably because there never were any special rates such as Flemings offered. Nary a canon or bishop in sight. Certainly there are no "fluffy old pussies," no decayed aristocrats, no impoverished members of the old county families. In fact, the fictional hotel never had Brown's clientele:

Queen Victoria, Napoleon, Teddy Roosevelt, Rudyard Kipling, Eleanor and Franklin Roosevelt all stayed at Brown's. Today, in the lounge, Italians, French and many Americans who think they have found the real thing, take proper afternoon tea (thankfully not erroneously called "high tea," the hot meal served in early evening when the numbers on the clock are high). Alas, none of the seed cake Lady Selina ordered at Bertram's is available since nowadays the only place the sesame-studded cake might be found is Harrods. Some things, however, remain the same: every variety of tea is on offer to accompany the selection of finger sandwiches, scones and pastries presented on a three-tiered tray, all replenished on request. If one is not too fussy about absolute accuracy, Brown's certainly makes one feel as if the real Bertram's has been identified.

Flemings or Brown's? A visit to these two Mayfair hotels may help decide which is the real Bertram's or perhaps conclude that Christie took bits of both and added some of her own touches.

Tube: Green Park.

22 Jermyn Street: Agatha Christie's brother, Louis Montant Miller, called Monty, did not figure very prominently in her life until after he returned to England. He was expected to die within six months from a wound suffered in World War I. In fact, he spent more time than that in London and then went on to a house the family bought for him in Dartmoor. He finally died much later in France tended by a nurse/companion. In her autobiography, Christie says that she was alternately maddened and fascinated by him. Though he seemed a failure, never succeeding at anything he tried, he was always cheerful and claimed he had enjoyed himself.

Upon his return from Africa, he convinced Agatha's brother-in-law, James Watts, to advance him money to build a prototype for a fleet of cargo boats. Instead, proving that he had "never been satisfied with anything but the best," he used the money to stay at an expensive hotel in Jermyn Street, the perfect location for him to stock up on pricey clothes, jewelry and bibelots.

Christie never identified the hotel but the private establishment known only as 22 Jermyn Street would surely suit Monty's requirements. The simple entrance between two exclusive shops hints at what is inside: an elegant, discreet hideaway offering luxurious, secure accommodation. The award-winning small hotel, consisting of 13 beautifully appointed suites and five studios, has been in the same family since 1915. This gem offers an opportunity for luxurious living very convenient to the best shops on Jermyn Street and Bond Street.

Tube: Piccadilly Circus.

Clubs: For Gentlemen, and Ladies Only on Occasion

VAD Ladies Club/The New Cavendish Club: Agatha Christie frequently mentions clubs. Lucy Eylesbarrow's club in *4:50 from Paddington/What Mrs. McGillicuddy Saw* was a typical London ladies club, a nondescript establishment that had one advantage—small, dark waiting rooms that were usually empty. This perhaps recalls Christie's own club where, according to a Mrs. de Silvo quoted in the *Daily Mail,* Agatha planned to spend the first night of her famous disappearance. Though Gwen Robyns, one of Christie's biographers, claims that she stayed at the Forum Club, that has not been verified. It's more likely that she used the VAD Ladies' Club. Founded by Lady Ampthill in 1920, it provided accommodation for the ladies who had served so valiantly in the Voluntary Aid Detachment.

The Club occupied premises at 28 Cavendish Square until 1957 when it moved to **44 Great Cumberland Place**. As it extended its membership to gentlemen as well as to women in business, the club's name was altered to the New Cavendish. Today, it is a safe and comfortable, moderately priced haven in the middle of London. The reception has a VAD recruiting poster from World War I when Agatha first joined the service. You almost expect to see Miss Marple comfortably settling into the overstuffed furniture in the lounge, enjoying the roof garden or having dinner in the upstairs restaurant. Indeed, the New Cavendish is so evocative of a Christie setting that Joan Hickson stayed there while filming the London portion of *The Mirror Crack'd*. A fan who would like to see the club that looks as if Agatha Christie belongs there needs a letter of introduction from a member or membership in a club with reciprocity.

Tube: Marble Arch.

Detection Club: Agatha, a long-time member of the Detection Club, served a term as ruler (president), though she took a somewhat irreverent attitude towards some of its rules and no doubt found the hocus-pocus of initiation amusing. Locating the club takes some doing. Founded in the '20s by classic mystery writer Anthony Berkeley so that mystery writers could discuss crime over dinner, it held its early meetings in rented rooms in Bohemian Soho, at 31 Gerrard St. After World War II, thanks to Dorothy Sayers, the club moved its meetings to Kingly Street behind Libertys. Twice yearly it has a dinner in a singularly unprepossessing building at **15 Garrick Street,** a favorite haunt of actors—not surprisingly, since the Garrick Club is named for the famous 18th-century actor David Garrick. The Garrick, with an eight-year waiting list of actors, writers and lawyers applying to join, excludes women; as recently as 1992, the Garrick voted 4–1 to keep them out, putting into action the sentiments of actor Derek Nimmo: "The only case for joining is to get away from women." Consequently, the Detection Club's biennial dinner there means that, though women may eat in the dining room in the evening, they cannot sit at the long members' table.

The Detection Club's initiation dinner, involving elaborate ceremony and exotic costumes, requires more elegant quarters. For that purpose, once a year, members dine at the Cafe Royal on the curve of the Regent Street Quadrant. This famous restaurant has been the haunt of notable artists and writers since Mr. Nicol opened it in 1865. Here you can eye the literati while sipping an original champagne cocktail: brandy, Grand Marnier, angostura bitters and champagne.

Tube: Piccadilly Circus.

Boodles: When anyone speaks of London clubs he usually means the gentlemen's clubs where members can gather to relax, drink and talk. Lord Catherham in *The Secret of Chimneys* was irritated that he had to "stand on the steps of the exclusive London club to which he belonged and listen to the interminable eloquence of the Hon. George Lomax." Membership in a good club is supposed to protect one from such inconveniences. Loyalty to his club is so vital that it is the last thing that a gentleman as impoverished as Major Porter in *Taken at the Flood* would consider giving up.

Thanks to his club, Canon Feather in *At Bertram's Hotel* at least had the pleasure of a good meal before his disappearance. He had dined early at the spectacular quasi-Grecian Athenaeum at 107 Pall Mall at Waterloo Place. This most famous of all the London clubs claimed as members Darwin, Dickens, Conrad, Kipling and many politicians and bishops. Its method of selecting members gave rise to the term "blackballing," a custom that made philosopher Bertrand Russell wait 40 years for admission.

The club to which Christie so enjoyed bringing her friends is Boodles, founded in 1762. Along with White's, the oldest club, and the Carlton, it lies around the corner from Pall Mall, at **28 St. James Street.** Its unpretentious facade has one distinguishing characteristic, a bow window added in 1824. It has always attracted members of the horsey set and country gentlemen, like Agatha's father, a member of New York's Union Club and a daily visitor to the Yacht Club in Torquay. Because like all the gentlemen's clubs Boodles employs an excellent chef, Agatha liked to entertain friends and family in its dining room, preferably ending the meal with her favorite dessert, Boodles Orange Fool. What she doesn't mention is that she could dine only when accompanied by a male Boodles member and then only in the ladies' side restaurant. The gentlemen's clubs' antediluvian policies, which seemed not to bother women of Christie's generation, today spark protests. So illustrious a member as Lord Anthony Lester resigned from the Garrick Club. Political scientist David Butler, a 42-year member whose grandfather founded the Oxford and Cambridge Club, resigned and the heads of the colleges at both institutions have written protests, to no avail.

The gentlemen's clubs have a number of seemingly odd customs. One club forbids taking paper out of one's pocket in the dining room; a member's wife was reprimanded when she took a wallpaper sample out of her bag to show her husband. In another club, the smoking room is the library, the dining room is called the coffee room but no coffee is served, and the Strangers Room is so called because in the early days non-members couldn't go into the coffee room. In 1885, Henry James entertained his guest, James McNeill Whistler, in the Strangers Room; now it is used mainly for privacy as when the Duke of Edinburgh recently dined with a member friend.

Though the elegantly unostentatious exteriors and the beautifully appointed interiors have not changed, the clubs have made certain changes. Most offer very reduced service on weekends because few members stay in town except for business. Beginning with the Reform Club, a number of clubs now admit women as members with full privileges. However, the Royal Automobile Club, next to the Reform Club on Pall Mall, bars women from the gentlemen's bar, the snooker room and the smoking room but allows them in the swimming pool. Some clubs have established reciprocity with American clubs, allowing not only strangers, but also foreigners full access. Perhaps now, Ian Fleming, the creator of the James Bond adventures, would not make the comments he did upon taking membership in Boodles: he explained that he expressly wanted to belong to a dull club, though he suggested his problem would have been to find one where anything really happened. However, the original purpose of clubs, to escape the hurley-burley, is still the same. As they did for Agatha Christie and her characters, the London clubs are a place where those of similar interests and backgrounds feel at home.

Tube: Green Park.

The St James Club: the only oddity about the St James is that, like Harry S Truman, it does not have a period in its name. Located behind the Ritz on Park Place where Agatha and Max had a serviced flat in World War II, the St James has adapted to changing times. It offers both full and temporary memberships to men and women of all nationalities. The imposing building at the end of a quiet cul-de-sac at **7–8 Park Place** has been luxuriously refurbished with every possible amenity in its 60 club rooms and suites. Foreign visitors particularly find its club-like atmosphere comforting. Though the St James has no Christie connection, save its location, its accessibility—if only to inquire about facilities—provides a nice look at club atmosphere.

Tube: Green Park.

Christie Works Mentioned in This Chapter

The ABC Murders
The Secret of Chimneys
Curtain
Witness for the Prosecution (play)
The Mousetrap (play)
The Mystery of the Blue Train
The Big Four
Thirteen for Dinner/Lord Edgware Dies
The Secret Adversary
Murder on the Orient Express
At Bertram's Hotel
4:50 from Paddington/What Mrs. McGillicuddy Saw
The Mirror Crack'd/The Mirror Crack'd from Side to Side
Taken at the Flood

Contacts and Resources for This Chapter

The Ritz Hotel, Piccadilly. Telephone: (0171) 493-8181, or in the United States 1-800-525-4800. *Tube:* Green Park.

Fortnum and Mason, 181 Piccadilly. Telephone: (0171) 734-8040. *Tube:* Green Park or Piccadilly Circus.

The Savoy Hotel, The Strand. Telephone: (0171) 836-4343. *Tube:* Charing Cross.

Claridges, Brook St., Mayfair. Telephone: (0171) 629-8860 or 1-800-223-6800. *Tube:* Bond St.

Flemings Hotel and Luxury Apartments, 7–12 Half Moon St., Mayfair. Telephone: (0171) 499-2964 or 1-800-348-4685. *Tube:* Green Park.

Brown's Hotel, Albemarle and Dover St., Mayfair. Telephone: (0171) 493-6020.

22 Jermyn St., St. James. Telephone: (0171) 734-2353 or 1-800-682-7808. *Tube:* Piccadilly Circus.

The New Cavendish Club, 44 Great Cumberland Place. Telephone: (0171) 723-0391. *Tube:* Marble Arch.

Cafe Royal, 68 Regent St. Telephone: (0171) 437-9090. *Tube:* Piccadilly Circus.

Athenaeum Club. 107 Pall Mall. *Tube:* Piccadilly Circus.

Boodles, 28 St. James St. *Tube:* Green Park.

The St James Club, 7–8 Park Place. Telephone: (0171) 629-7688 or 1-800-877-0447. *Tube:* Green Park.

No Christie Connections But Tried and True

Wren at St. James, 197 Piccadilly SW1. Telephone: (0171) 437-9419. No credit cards. Vegetarian. Great soups. *Tube:* Green Park or Piccadilly Circus.

Royal Academy of Arts Restaurant, Piccadilly, W1. Telephone: (0171) 439-7438. *Tube:* Piccadilly Circus.

Museum Tavern, 49 Great Russell St., WC1. Telephone: (0171) 242-8987. Directly across from the British Museum. Reasonable and friendly. *Tube:* Tottenham Court Rd.

Red Lion Pub, 2 Duke of York St. off Jermyn St., SW1. Telephone: (0171) 930-2030. No credit cards. Great fish and chips Saturday only. *Tube:* Piccadilly Circus.

Sherlock Holmes Pub and Restaurant (upstairs) 10 Northumberland St., WC1. Telephone: (0171) 930-2644. A bobby recommended this one! *Tube:* Charing Cross or Embankment.

Cittie of Yorke, 22–23 High Holborn, WC1. Telephone: (0171) 242-7670. Barristers, judges, financial types. Great atmosphere. *Tube:* Holborn or Chancery Lane.

King's Head and Eight Bells, 50 Cheyne Walk, SW3. Telephone: (0171) 352-1820. *Tube:* Sloane Square.

Ye Olde Cheshire Cheese. Wine Office Court, 145 Fleet St., EC4. Telephone: (0171) 353-6170. An historic pub and three dining rooms. Very English food. *Tube:* St. Paul's.

Sofra Restaurant. Shepherd's Market, Mayfair. Telephone: (0171) 493-3320. Fresh Turkish food, very good value. *Tube:* Green Park.

Tea: Hyde Park Hotel, 66 Knightsbridge, SW1. Telephone: (0171) 235-2000. Queen Mother Elizabeth took the princesses here for tea. Just steps from Harrods, this is my favorite place for tea in all of London.

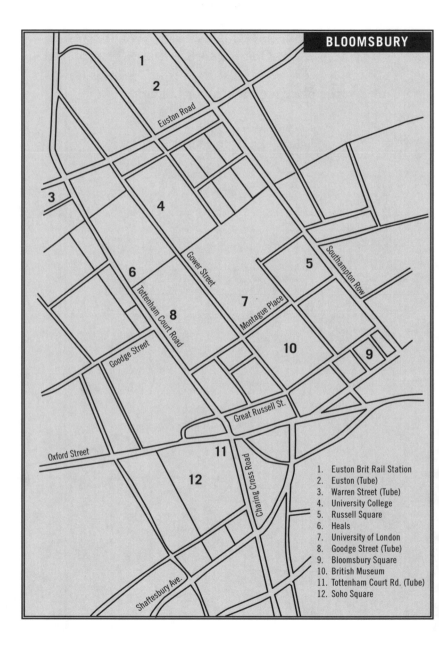

BLOOMSBURY

1. Euston Brit Rail Station
2. Euston (Tube)
3. Warren Street (Tube)
4. University College
5. Russell Square
6. Heals
7. University of London
8. Goodge Street (Tube)
9. Bloomsbury Square
10. British Museum
11. Tottenham Court Rd. (Tube)
12. Soho Square

4

The British Museum

LIKE A CLUE in one of Agatha Christie's mysteries, Object No. 127412 proves elusive. It should be on display in the British Museum's Gallery 58, but the room may be in need of cleaning; the entire group of galleries may be closed for rearrangement or for lack of staff; it may even be off on one of its many journeys as when it recently traveled for three years on loans to several museums. To compound its mystery, Object No. 127412 is variously identified. The 1992 revised edition of *Treasures of the British Museum* calls it "Lioness Mauling an African." But the Department of Western Asiatic Antiquities describes it as "lioness devouring a negro in a thicket." Christie's husband, Sir Max Mallowan, its discoverer, says it is "a savage lioness mauling a dark 'Ethiopian.'" But tracking down the carved four-inch-square ivory, jewel-encrusted panel from Nimrud's northwestern palace is well worth the effort both for its own sake and as an example of the depth of the mystery writer we know and love.

Agatha met her second husband Max in 1930 on a dig with the Woolleys. After their marriage, she accompanied him to the Near East once a year from 1932–60, except during the war years. She claimed she could write anywhere, even in the most difficult conditions. All she needed was a flat surface and her trusty Remington typewriter. Her imagination and creativity never deserted her. Her description of life on a dig, *Come, Tell Me How You Live*, is a tribute to the joys of exploration. Her own work seemed inspired by the finds. In the desert, she worked on her novels and began her autobiography. Treasures unearthed made her reflect on how proud she was to be part of the human race.

She and Max made a fine working team. Both had a highly refined aesthetic sense and the ability to communicate their appreciation. He describes the lioness plaque in words of deep sensuality. The victim, in "the embrace of death,... proffers his neck ... as if in the ecstasy of sacrifice." The lioness has a "sinuous outline." He describes the gorgeous contrasting background: "a meadow of Egyptian 'lilies' and papyrus flowers with golden stems, blue and red in alternate rows, bending now one way, now the other, as if swaying before the wind." Christie's more direct description has a slightly different focus: the Negro "lies there, in a golden loincloth, gold points in his hair, and his head is lifted in what seems like ecstasy as the lioness stands over him for the kill."

They shared, too, a reverence for and a desire to preserve the past. Agatha was always a full participant on a dig. She helped wash the sludge of 25,000 years off the largest ivory head ever found, the Lady of the Well. She used her knitting needles, orange sticks and cold cream to clean jewelry, pottery and ivories. She kept wet towels on ivories to prevent the damage caused if they dried too quickly. Max recorded his finds and drew important conclusions about ancient Assyria in scholarly books. She incorporated her knowledge in her best-selling books, allowing even a casual reader a chance to learn a good deal about the Ancient Near East from her autobiography or her account of life on a dig, *Come, Tell Me How You Live*. In *Murder in Mesopotamia*, an early Akkadian cemetery, tells (mounds), ancient pottery, cylinder seals, cleaning agents like hydrochloric acid—all play a role.

The British Museum devotes a good deal of space to the Assyrian discoveries. The little objects, like the lioness ivory, jewelry and pottery, are upstairs in rooms 51–59. Soon the lioness ivory will have the place it deserves in a refurbished gallery. The cylinder seals occupy rooms 54 and 55. But the ground floor rooms devoted to the large antiquities from Western Asia are spectacular. Indeed, they rival the Greek collection both for size and beauty. They fill rooms 16–21, 24 and 26. The great finds from the Nimrud Palace in room 20 made Max's reputation. Most stunning is the huge winged, human-headed bull that guarded the palace.

A visit to the British Museum provides a broader view of Christie's talents and her marriage to Max. Be sure to see the Elgin marbles that vie with the Nimrud treasures for pride of place. And just across the street is the Museum Tavern, one of the best in London.

Tube: Tottenham Court Rd.

Christie Works Mentioned in This Chapter

Come, Tell Me How You Live
An Autobiography
Murder in Mesopotamia

Contacts and Resources for This Chapter

The British Museum, Great Russell St. Telephone: (0171) 636-1555. Recorded Information: (0171) 580-1788. Monday through Saturday 10 a.m. to 5 p.m.; Sunday 2:30 p.m. to 6 p.m. (galleries must clear 10 minutes before closing); closed 3 days at Christmas, New Year's Day, Good Friday and bank holidays. *Tube:* Holborn, Tottenham Court Rd., Russell Square.

Museum Tavern, 49 Great Russell St. Telephone: (0171) 242-8987. *Tube:* Holborn, Tottenham Court Rd., Russell Square.

Part II

Venturing
Beyond London

5

Trains

Trains have always been one of my favorite things. It is sad nowadays that one no longer has engines that seem to be one's personal friends.

NO READER OF Agatha Christie's works doubts the truth of that statement. In her autobiography, she recalls pretending her favorite childhood toy—a hoop—was a train; as engine driver, conductor or passenger, she rode around the grounds of Ashfield, her family home, on three imaginary lines: The Tubular, The Tub and the Terrace. Trains figure prominently in her books. Arrival and departure times establish alibis and a means of escape for the murderer. Cleverly maneuvered timetables provide the opportunity for crime as in *The ABC Murders.* Who can forget *What Mrs. McGillicuddy Saw!* when she took *The 4:50 from Paddington*, or what happened to Mr. Ratchett on the Orient Express.

Since Christie last wrote about Poirot and Miss Marple journeying by train, stations have been rebuilt and trains have been modernized. The infamous Lord Beeching, Minister of Transportation, eliminated many profitable branch lines in the '50s. And British Rail no longer exists as an entity. Privatization has created a mass of separate companies, all with names no one recognizes: Thames Link? Wales and West? Each serves a different part of the United Kingdom, making coordination difficult.

Though unstaffed, many of the lovely Victorian railway stations have been preserved, such as the one at Torquay, Christie's hometown, with ornamental woodwork and cast iron. (It still operates at full staff.) Old carriages like those Miss Marple rode are hauled by locomotives on some excursion routes off the main lines. Preserved railways use steam engines; one of these, the Paignton and Dartmouth Railway, runs through the scenic Dart Valley near Greenway House, Christie's home where her daughter Rosalind Hicks lives. And despite the seemingly ubiquitous automobile, trains still play an important role in life here. The train traveler can capture easily the true feeling of what still lingers of Agatha Christie's England.

Paddington Station, without the Bear, serves as a good case in point. Since she lived much of her life in the southern section of the West Country, Christie set many of her novels there. Her characters constantly "to-and-fro" between London and fictional locations. They most often catch their trains at Paddington Station, a memorial to Isambard Kingdom Brunel, known as the world's greatest engineer. He planned and personally supervised every aspect of the Great Western Railway's construction. Originally built to haul ore from the tin and copper mines of Cornwall, the GWR also developed the large-scale tourist trade that helped create Christie's beloved English Riviera in Devon.

Despite additions and modernization, Paddington Station

has retained its original style. The train shed has a glazed three-bay cover inspired by the naves and transepts of a cathedral and by the Crystal Palace, the hall for the Great Exhibition of 1851. The French baroque Great Western Royal Hotel, forming the front of the station, features a pediment of sculptured Victorian virtues and a stylish Art Deco GWR monogram. Fittingly, a larger than life-sized statue of a seated Brunel faces the departure board in this most exciting of the London stations.

Christie's characters often fretted over their journey. They knew that travel by train takes a little planning. Along with a butler who knew the trains by heart, every Victorian household had a Bradshaw's Monthly Railway Guide. Because it listed all the stations in alphabetical order, passengers shortened the title to "The ABC," a sobriquet Christie used for *The ABC Murders*.

Today's train traveler is no different. Though they (and you) probably don't have the indulgence of a butler for planning, there is the Intercity Guide to Services. Leaflets for routes served by a specific major station are available free at information booths, but nor for the connecting services. Charts are so complicated that even seasoned British Rail passengers can be stymied. Ticket agents at manned stations make good substitutes for that vanished breed of servant, but many stations are staffed part time or not at all. One efficient way to plan a journey is to use a travel agency that displays a rail logo. Using a computer program similar to that used for air travel, the agent can take the time to work out the most complicated journey at the most economical round trip fare ("return" or "same day return"), and can save the traveler the nuisance of holding up the queue at the station ticket window. However, fewer and fewer travel agencies handle rail travel as the break-up of British Rail has made such work unprofitable. Barred access to a major station or a willing travel agent, a potential traveler must use the telephone service for rail travel. Knowledgeable, patient, and efficient agents are on duty 24 hours a day, 7 days a week to advise on routes, schedules, and reservations.

Miss Brewis in *Dead Man's Folly* expressed her concern about Poirot's trip from Paddington to Nassecombe: "I do hope you didn't have too crowded a journey. The trains are sometimes terrible this time of year." British Rail has invented a scheme that helps circumvent that bane of its passengers. It recommends seat reservations especially on certain peak days, holidays or summer Saturdays. Travelers to the West Country will want a seat on the left side of the train for best views of the scenery. Passengers have the option to specify a "facing" seat to prevent the queasiness that results for some people riding backward. With carriages lettered and seats numbered, in theory a passenger with a reserved seat can stand in a likely spot on the platform; however, even the stationmaster cannot always predict the ordering of the carriages or where a particular carriage will stop.

Older carriages, relics from the days when station porters opened and closed the doors for passengers, have no handles on the inside. The uninitiated may find themselves riding beyond a station, unaware that these doors open by sliding down the window and turning the handle on the outside. Such outward opening doors explain the posters on board exhorting, "Please don't open the carriage door until the train has stopped," as well as those in the station that advise waiting passengers to stand well back from the platform edge.

A further danger awaits the unwary: both older and

smaller stations have short platforms. To avoid a tumble, passengers without seat reservations need to be sure they are riding in a car that will stop at the platform, information best obtained from the guard (conductor) before boarding. Inquiry also can prevent being in the wrong half of a train that divides for two different destinations.

Luggage can be dealt with efficiently. Though train porters have become an endangered species except in the larger stations, as Miss Marple noted in *Murder with Mirrors/They Do It with Mirrors*, British Rail thoughtfully provides, free of charge, large numbers of luggage trolleys (baggage carts). They can be found at the entrances to stations and on every platform, though never near the door you exit the train. Nearly every station has a lift (elevator) so passengers need not lug suitcases up flights of stairs. Probably because trains predate the fashion for packing lightly, they have ample space in addition to the overhead racks for stowing luggage. Nearly every carriage has a shelved storage area just inside the door; passengers can neatly stack suitcases there knowing they will be safe. Some carriages have cunningly-shaped triangular spaces between back-to-back seats that hold all but the largest cases. Some trains even have baggage cars for truly oversized items such as bicycles.

Using Saver or off-peak fares, passengers can treat themselves to first class, perhaps in a compartment on an older train, just as Luke Fitzwilliam and the observant but doomed Miss Fullerton did in *Murder Is Easy/Easy to Kill*. But second class is quite comfortable, especially if the carriages feature handy tables between pairs of facing seats. A train may offer food in a restaurant car, in a buffet car (pronounced "buffy," but only on trains), or from trolleys similar to those on airplanes. In any class of travel, aboard carriages of any vintage, train travelers are guaranteed unforgettable close-ups of Agatha Christie's England.

Christie Works Mentioned in This Chapter

The ABC Murders
4:50 from Paddington/What Mrs. McGillicuddy Saw!
Murder on the Orient Express
Dead Man's Folly
Murder with Mirrors/They Do It with Mirrors
Murder Is Easy/Easy to Kill

Contacts and Resources for This Chapter

Rail Travel Inquiries. Telephone: (0345) 48-49-50 for information on national train services, facilities, and fares, 24 hours a day, 7 days a week.

UK Rail Tickets. Telephone: (0345) 12-56-25. For ticket purchase and seat reservations by mail charged to a credit card. 8 a.m. to 8 p.m. 7 days a week.

Paddington Station, Praed St. Telephone: (0171) 262-6767. For trains to West of England, South Midlands, South Wales.

Charing Cross Station, Strand. Telephone: (0171) 928-5100. For trains to southern England.

Euston Station, Euston Rd. Telephone: (0171) 387-7070. For trains to the Midlands, North Wales, northwest England, west coast of Scotland.

Kings Cross Station, Euston Rd. Telephone: (0171) 278-2477. For trains to West Yorkshire, Northeast England, east coast of Scotland.

Liverpool Street Station, Bishopsgate. Telephone: (0171) 928-5100. For trains to east and northeast London, Essex and East Anglia.

Victoria Station, Buckingham Palace Rd. Telephone: (0171) 928-5100. For trains to Gatwick, southwest England and the Continent.

Waterloo Station, Waterloo Rd. Telephone: (0171) 928-5100. Trains for the south of England and the Eurostar to Paris.

BritRail 1-888-274-7245

By mail: 226–230 Westchester Ave., White Plains, NY 10604

In person: BritRail's British Travel Shop, 551 Fifth Ave. (at 45th St.), New York, NY 10176.

The Orient Express

AGATHA CHRISTIE MADE her first trip on the Orient Express almost on a whim in 1928. Following her mother's death, her own famous disappearance, a divorce from Archie and daughter Rosalind's departure for school, she found herself somewhat at loose ends. Two days before she had planned to leave on a therapeutic trip to the West Indies, she met Commander and Mrs. Howe at a dinner party. They spoke engagingly of their recent trip to Baghdad. Recalling that she had always felt a faint attraction to archaeology, and remembering a recent article in the *Times* about Leonard Woolley's Mesopotamian excavations at Ur, Agatha became enthusiastic. When she learned that the journey did not require travel by ship (she suffered violently from *mal de mer*) but was made on the Orient Express, Christie knew she would go. As she said in her autobiography, she had always wanted to travel on the Orient Express. Whenever she had seen the train standing at Calais, she longed to climb aboard.

The next day, she canceled her tickets for the West Indies and scheduled her trip on the Simplon-Orient-Express to Stamboul (as Istanbul/Constantinople was commonly called);

from Stamboul to Damascus on the Eastern extension of the Orient Express, the Taurus Express; and across the desert by bus to Baghdad. Thus, Christie began what she called in her autobiography, her "Second Spring."

From her own experiences on the train, she probably got the idea for Poirot's comment, "It lends itself to romance, my friend.... For three days these people, these strangers ... are brought together." When she traveled alone, a suitable male always found time to help her. In the early '30s, as Max related in his memoirs, Agatha almost had a "final" adventure with the train just before beginning *Murder on the Orient Express*. She nearly did not live to write her most celebrated book. At Calais, she slipped on the icy platform and fell beneath the train; a porter rescued her before the train started moving.

On the return journey from her second visit to Ur, she and her future husband Max Mallowan fell in love. They took a honeymoon trip on the Orient Express, and they traveled on it almost every year until the innovation of convenient air travel.

In Christie's day, rather than making their own way to Calais, English travelers could begin their journey at Victoria Station aboard the Golden Arrow train in a luxurious Pullman day carriage. Agatha said that she and Max always went by Pullman to Dover because of Max's book-filled suitcases, which he feared would go astray if relegated to a baggage car. After crossing the Channel by steamer, passengers would find the *Flèche d'Or*, the Continental Pullman counterpart of the Golden Arrow, waiting with the deluxe Wagon-Lit sleeper designated for their individual destinations: Bucharest via Vienna; Venice and Trieste; Athens; Istanbul. Christie described her feelings when she climbed aboard: "I entered my Wagon-Lit compartment at Calais, the journey to Dover and the tiresome sea voyage disposed of, and settled comfortably into the train of my dreams."

"The Train of Kings, the King of Trains," as it became known, offered every luxury, including a fourgon-lit serving as a bath and shower/bath car—until Istanbul, that is. On the other side of the Bosporus, another train entirely, the Taurus Express, carried the passengers to Damascus. On this segment of the journey, Agatha suffered what she called a short spell of bad luck. Bed bugs crawled from the walls of the old-fashioned wooden railway carriages. Violently allergic to their bites, she ran a high fever accompanied by swelling in her limbs. Ironically, the same thing happened on her honeymoon trip. On later journeys, she carried a little tin of bug powder to sprinkle on the woodwork, much to the amazement and amusement of the Turkish customs officials who suspected her of smuggling drugs.

Passengers on today's Venice Simplon-Orient-Express need not worry about suffering Christie's discomfort. Thanks to American entrepreneur and railroad enthusiast James B. Sherwood, over 35 vintage sleepers, Pullmans and restaurant cars have been restored to a grand and luxurious standard exceeding the Orient Express, even at the height of its fame. Just as in Christie's day, passengers board a brown and cream Pullman at Victoria Station, on Track 1 or 2 after some welcoming refreshment in a track-side lounge. Then they cross the Channel to climb aboard the blue and gold carriages of the Continental train at Boulogne, bound for Paris, Verona and Venice.

But a traveler need not leave England to experience a journey on Agatha's favorite train. From January to November, the British section of the Venice Simplon-Orient-Express offers day excursions around some of the English country-side's most picturesque areas in day Pullman carriages like the one used in the film *Murder on the Orient Express*. On trips to places such as Salisbury, Leeds Castle, Bath or Dover, passengers ride in sumptuous carriages featuring inlaid paneling, brass fittings, crystal chandeliers, pink silk lamp shades and velvet-upholstered wing chairs protected by handmade lace antimacassars. Liveried attendants serve beautifully prepared food on tables laid with bone china and silver flatware. The richly decorated and paneled lavatory in each carriage includes a mosaic floor illustrating the mythological character whose name the carriage bears, such as Cygnus, Ibis or Minerva.

Passengers look the part: men wear coats and ties, many women wear hats and gloves. They form a group as diverse as those found in the famous mystery. On a typical journey a traveler can find families, honeymooners, parties of friends, a Michael Jackson look-alike wearing red sequins, or a very expensive Teddy Bear, Happy, sporting a lace bib as he travels with his owners to raise funds for sick children. Anyone fortunate enough to be on the Orient Express on September 15, 1990, would have seen the most distinguished passengers of all, Hercule Poirot (David Suchet) and Miss Marple (Joan Hickson). In celebration of the Agatha Christie Centenary, they traveled to her birthplace, Torquay, for tea on the Imperial Hotel's terrace, the setting for Miss Marple's explanation of the solution in *Sleeping Murder,* her last case. Expensive and worth it, the Orient Express is the quintessential Christie experience. Ride it back in time for the mystery, the romance, not to mention the fun of history brought to life.

Train: Victoria Station.

Christie Works Mentioned in This Chapter

Murder on the Orient Express
Sleeping Murder

Contacts and Resources for This Chapter

Venice Simplon-Orient-Express Ltd., Sea Containers House, 20 Upper Ground, London SE1 9PF. Telephone: (0171) 928-6000. In the United States: 1-800-524-2420.

HARROGATE

Skipton Rd. A59

East Parade

North Park Road

Station Parade

James Street

3

Kings Road

Kings Road

Springfield Ave.

1

Parliament Street

Prospect Hill

Swan Road

Crescent Road

5

Cold Bath Road

4

2

York Road

Cornwall Road

6

Valley Drive

1. International Centre
2. Old Swan Hotel
3. Bus and Rail Station
4. Royal Pump Room Museum
5. Royal Baths
6. Valley Gardens
   Winter Gardens
7. The Stray

7

Harrogate:
Where the Lady Vanished

O N THE NIGHT of December 3, 1926, Agatha Christie disappeared, creating her most baffling mystery. Her beloved grey bottle-nosed Morris car, containing her fur coat and a small packed bag, was found lodged in a thick hedge and precariously balanced over a chalk pit near Newlands Pond in Surrey. The car was near the spot where her husband, Col. Archibald Christie, and his mistress, Nancy Neele, were spending a weekend.

Eleven days later, Christie's husband came to collect her from the elegant Yorkshire spa town of Harrogate. Her movements from the time she left the car until she registered at the Harrogate Hydropathic Hotel as Mrs. Teresa Neele remain largely unaccounted for; her motives for disappearing and her state of mind have prompted all kinds of speculation. Doctors stated she suffered an amnesiac fugue brought on by the strain of her deteriorating marriage and her mother's death.

Christie's official biographer, Janet Morgan, deduced that she somehow made her way to Guildford railway station and took a milk train to London's Waterloo Station. After purchasing a coat, a small case and some night things at Whiteleys Department Store in London, she took a late morning train from either Kings Cross or St. Pancras Station. Perhaps she chose Harrogate because she saw a poster at Waterloo Station advertising the spa. In fact, Harrogate resemblanced Torquay, the Devon resort town where she had grown up. She had also mentioned in a letter that Harrogate would be a nice place to visit.

Agatha took a taxi from the station to the Hydro Hotel, now known by its original name, the Old Swan. Today's guests enter just as she did through the beautifully polished wood and brass revolving door. The reception area and lounge have undergone considerable change since the evening of December 14, 1926, when Archie Christie waited nearly an hour for the first glimpse of his wife since her disappearance; however, the staircase she descended and the lift watched carefully by police remain directly opposite the entrance. The Christies acknowledged each other and, as if nothing were amiss, dined in the hotel dining room (now called the Wedgwood Room) with its splendid ceiling and beautiful paneling. Today, guests have a second choice: to dine downstairs in the more intimate Agatha Christie Library Restaurant with its Art Deco glass and *trompe l'oeil* bookshelves. Though the press was told that the Christies shared a room that night, Archie did not join Agatha in number 5, but occupied number 10; today, neither room can be positively located because of continuous remodeling.

Agatha enjoyed many pastimes at Harrogate, particularly the dancing in the Winter Gardens. There, a part-time banjo player, Bob Tappin, recognized her. Members of the hotel staff later said they, too, had guessed her identity, but discreetly protected her in keeping with the hotel's policy of honoring a guest's privacy. However, Robert Barnard, the mystery writer and Christie scholar, maintains that such stories were creations of the popular press.

The Royal Baths Assembly Rooms, a few blocks from the hotel, are now open only for conferences. But the Turkish Baths in the building still operate seven days a week though, thankfully, the electric shock baths are no longer part of the regime. Nearby, the domed, octagon-shaped Royal Pump Room has been converted into a museum of spa history and local curios where the daring can sample the nauseating sulfurous waters. The touted invigorating powers of these waters drew crowds to Harrogate from Victorian times until after World War II.

Along Harrogate's broad, tree-lined streets, many of the fashionable shops that tempted the landed gentry in the heyday of the spa are now outnumbered by equally fashionable antique shops. The city has earned the reputation as England's Floral Town, thanks to a number of awards and the Harrogate Spring Flower Festival in late April. Visitors can stroll through the Stray, the 200 acres of horseshoe-shaped greensward, protected by the Enclosure Act of 1770 for the benefit of the public. They can promenade through the Valley Gardens or rest in the shelter of the long glass-covered Sun Colonnade as the author of *All Creatures Great and Small*, the late James Harriot, did on his days away from his veterinary practice. No visit to Harrogate would be complete without an afternoon tea at Betty's Cafe on Parliament Street. Founded in 1919 by a Swiss confectioner, Betty's serves superb pastries, heavily laden with the thick cream Agatha Christie so loved. No doubt she enjoyed a few during her vanishing act.

Train: Kings Cross Station to Harrogate via York.

Contacts and Resources for This Chapter

Harrogate Tourist Information Centre, Royal Baths Assembly Rooms, Crescent Rd. Harrogate, HG1 2RR. Telephone: (01423) 537-357.

Betty's Cafe Tearoom, 1 Parliament St. Telephone: (01423) 569-861.

Turkish Sauna Suite, Royal Baths Assembly Rooms, Crescent Rd. Telephone: (01423) 562-498. Open seven days a week.

Pump Room Museum, Crown Place. Telephone: (01423) 503-340. Monday through Saturday 10 a.m. to 5 p.m., Sunday 2 p.m. to 5 p.m., April through October; November through March closes at 4 p.m.

Old Swan Hotel, Swan Road, Harrogate, HG1 2SR. Telephone: (01423) 500-055.

No Christie Connections But Tried and True

Russell Hotel, Valley Drive, Harrogate, HG2 0JN. Telephone: (01423) 509-866.

8

The Island Sanctuary

IN THE 1930s the rich and the famous found a secret island hideaway just off the coast of Devon in South Hams at Bigbury-on-Sea. Members of the smart set, who came to Burgh Island to escape the press and to frolic in privacy, reputedly included Lord Montbattan, Noel Coward and Edward Prince of Wales with Wallis Simpson. Sir Max Mallowan, the renowned archaeologist and his wife, the more renowned mystery writer Agatha Christie, came to vacation. The island and hotel inspired two of her novels, *Evil Under the Sun* and *Ten Little Indians/And Then There Were None*. They stayed at the Burgh Island Hotel, a great white palace commissioned by Archibald Nettlefold, a steel magnate and owner of the Comedy Theatre that staged Agatha Christie's plays in London. Those jet setters of the day took seriously the advice of the great travel writer, S. P. B. Mais:

> *Like the seabirds you can fly over to mingle with the workaday world when you like, but you can also fly back when you like to your noiseless dustless Island Sanctuary.*

The resident band, the Mayfair Four, led by Harry Roy whose fans called him "The Little Hotcha-Ma-Cha-Cha," were rowed out to the diving platform in the center of the Mermaid Natural Rock Pool to entertain the guests as they enjoyed their cocktails at water's edge. In those days, the Pimms Cups and the champagne to accompany the caviar had to be rushed over by waiters from the nearby Pilchard Inn since the hotel had no bar. The *cordon bleu*-trained kitchen staff came from all over Europe.

The rules were very strict: no dogs, no children, black tie for men and evening dress for women at dinner, and no questions about who arrived with whom. The rumor that Nettlefold had bought the island for his mistress enhanced the resort's racy reputation. Old legends of thieves and smugglers abounded. The Elizabethan pirate Tom Crocker, shot dead by a "preventative officer's" pistol, supposedly haunted the island.

Following its wartime requisition and subsequent sale, the property fell into disrepair until by chance in late 1985, fashion consultants Beatrice and Tony Porter heard about the 1929 Art Deco-style hotel on an island convenient to London. The Porters have restored the hotel to its former glory, including the stained glass Peacock Dome over the Palm Court, and the parquet flooring in the Sun Lounge. Authentic period pieces make up the hotel's furnishings. The addition of a '20s bar means no one need wait for drinks as guests did in the old days. The hotel serves Devon cream teas in the Sun Lounge as well as dinner in the magnificent Ballroom. Proper attire is still required. The Porters offer the kind of recreation that made Burgh Island Hotel a playground before the war: snooker, table tennis, walking paths, the secret beach completely surrounded by towering rocks, every sort of water sport and, of course, dancing.

Though the Porters have added a heliport with service from Heathrow, most guests will come to Bigbury-on-Sea by car, following the same route as the guests in Agatha Christie's *Ten Little Indians/And Then There Were None*. After a series of winding narrow country roads, visitors come up steep Folly Hill to Folly Farm. They take the zigzag track toward the shore with no chance to re-create the approach made by one of Agatha Christie's characters, Anthony Marsten in *Ten Little Indians* who looked like "a Hero God out of some Northern Saga" when he roared up in his fantastically powerful car. On a fine summer day, the thick traffic on the narrow road forces drivers to give way to oncoming traffic. The road doesn't go any farther than the cliff's edge and ends in a car park run on the honor system: pay a pound at the little cafe but no one ever comes to check.

Nor do today's visitors bound for the island have need for the motor launch Christie's characters required when they headed for the Jolly Roger Hotel in *Evil under the Sun*. Twice a day the tide ebbs, allowing passage by foot over a causeway; when the waters rise again, an ungainly giant sea tractor, driven until recently by Jimbo, plies the waves on the half hour for 50p.

The elegant hotel and Burgh Island make up for the inauspicious introduction. The captain's cabin of the last sailing vessel to be a flagship of the Royal Navy, *The Ganges*, is attached to the hotel's facade, making an eerie sight on a moonlit night. By day, light streams into the hotel windows and the glass walls of the Sun Lounge, and filters through the Peacock Dome's glass onto the green wicker furniture in the Palm Court. Each of the 14 suites, named for a famous guest and suitably furnished with unusual examples of Art

Deco, has magnificent sea views.

The island offers much to explore: the ruins of an ancient monastery, the remains of the Huer's Hut named for the look-out who raised the hue and cry to alert fishermen that a school of fish approached, the bird sanctuary on Little Island, precipitous cliffs overlooking the surf-pounded jagged rocks that have claimed so many wrecks, and a veritable sun-trap on a secret beach exactly like the one where Arlena Marshall met her death in *Evil Under the Sun*.

Because the hotel had not yet been restored in 1982, the film version of *Evil Under the Sun* starring Peter Ustinov was made in Yugoslavia. But just a few hours from London at South Devon's Burgh Island Hotel, Agatha Christie readers can find the genuine glamour and mystery that inspired her. No doubt it will inspire you as well.

By Train: London, Paddington Station to Totnes or Plymouth—3 hours; taxi to the island—30 minutes

Non-residents can book for lunch, cocktails or dinner. Telephone: (01548) 810514. In keeping with its reputation for discretion, the hotel does not offer facilities for the casual visitor. But you can always get refreshment at the Pilchard Inn on the island.

Christie Works Mentioned in This Chapter

Evil Under the Sun
Ten Little Indians/And Then There Were None

Contacts and Resources for This Chapter

Burgh Island Hotel, Bigbury-on-Sea, South Devon TQ7 4BG.
Telephone: (01548) 810-514.

9

Torquay

A GATHA CHRISTIE DEVOTES the first two chapters of her autobiography to a loving description of her childhood in Torquay. She pays tribute to that time in her life in *Evil Under the Sun*. When Poirot asks Rosamund Darnley if she had a very English childhood, she replies

> *Oh incredibly so! The country—a big shabby house—horses, dogs—walks in the rain—wood fires—apples in the orchard—lack of money—old tweeds—evening dresses that went on from year to year—a neglected garden—with Michaelmas daisies coming out like big banners in the Autumn.*

Torquay today is not quite country. It is the capital of Devon's south coast, the English Riviera. Indeed, even when Agatha's parents, Clara and Frederick Miller, first arrived in the late 19th century, Torquay offered other attractions besides the villa they purchased in the country high above the harbor. It had lovely weather, sea front parks, palm trees, fine hotels, marvelous swimming beaches and best of all, a social life satisfying enough for a comfortably situated gentleman and his family. Through the years, it became more and more pop-

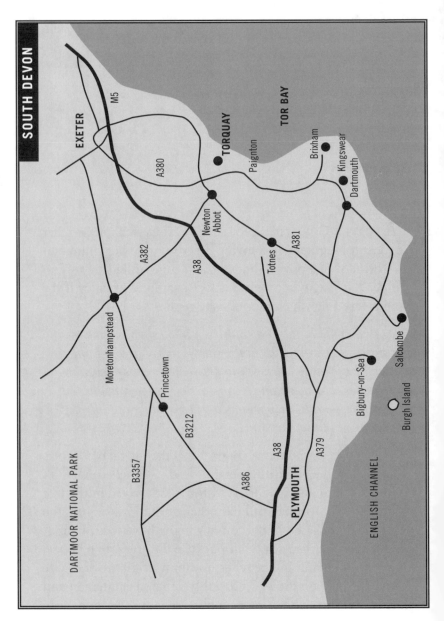

ular for those who enjoyed salubrious surroundings, particularly if they were over 65, as Lady Lucy Angkatell comments in *The Hollow*.

A visit to Agatha Christie's birthplace requires some effort, particularly as a day trip from London. However, it promises many rewards: The town is attractive, it holds much to see in addition to the Christie sites, and the journey itself involves a variety of transport—train, steam train, riverboat and ferry—through some spectacular venues.

The trip from Paddington Station to Totnes takes about three hours. This attractive town, though it has no Christie connections, is fascinating. On market day, the citizens don gorgeous Elizabethan costumes. The pleasant path from the station to the riverside winds past a castle and through narrow streets lined with a good range of buildings from the 15th century onwards. The cruise from Totnes down the River Dart duplicates that in *Dead Man's Folly*. The route goes past the village of Dittisham (pronounced "ditsam"). It has a statue honoring the Belgian war refugees who inspired Christie's choice of nationality for her little mustachioed detective. The boathouse where the body is found in *Dead Man's Folly* is easy to spot, though its thatched roof has been replaced with something more substantial. But passengers need a sharp eye to catch a glimpse of Greenway House, which Agatha purchased in 1938 as a summer home, high in the dense trees that line the shore. Agatha's daughter, Rosalind Hicks, lives there now. Though the house is not open to the public, a charity tea and plant sale are held at its gardens in April.

The pleasant one-hour journey ends at Dartmouth, the setting for the short story, "The Regatta Mystery"; a diamond heist occurs at the Royal George Hotel. Both the Britannia

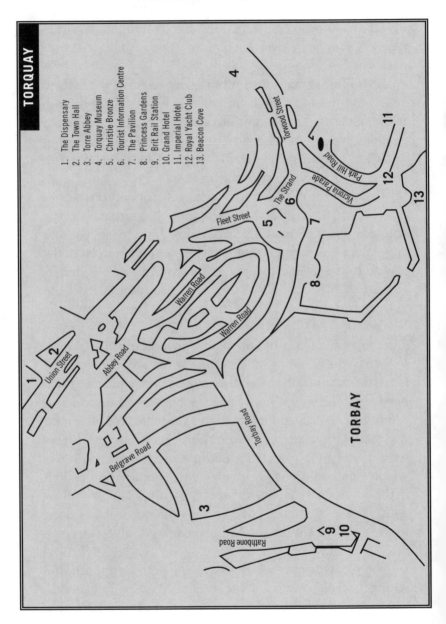

TORQUAY

1. The Dispensary
2. The Town Hall
3. Torre Abbey
4. Torquay Museum
5. Christie Bronze
6. Tourist Information Centre
7. The Pavilion
8. Princess Gardens
9. Brit Rail Station
10. Grand Hotel
11. Imperial Hotel
12. Royal Yacht Club
13. Beacon Cove

Union Street

Abbey Road

Belgrave Road

Warren Road

Warren Road

Fleet Street

Torbay Road

Rathbone Road

The Strand

Victoria Parade

Torwood Street

Park Hill Road

TORBAY

Royal Naval College and Dartmouth Castle are worth a visit. A stroll along Dartmouth's steep streets rewards with views of the harbor from which 33,000 Americans disembarked in 1944 for the D-Day invasion of Normandy.

The 10-minute ferry ride from Dartmouth to Kingswear costs 50p. The Paignton and Dartmouth Railway runs a beautifully restored steam train from Kingswear. The AA *See Britain by Train Guide* claims that no other line offers such spectacular views. From high above the Dart estuary, the line plunges into the quarter-mile Greenway Tunnel. Passengers may disembark at Churston to visit what Christie called "a beautiful little church" in the parish that includes Greenway House. Struck by how the "plain glass east window gaped … like a gap in teeth," she had a glass window installed in her favorite mauve and green. She loved looking at it on Sundays and felt that its simple design with the Good Shepherd would stand the test of time.

After Churston, the line begins to dip as it crosses the spectacular Hookhills and Broadsands viaducts. Exmouth is visible as well as occasional glimpses of the contrasting red cliffs of Devon and white cliffs of Dover. The end of the run follows the South Downs Coast Path as it skirts Tor Bay. The restored line ends at Paignton where passengers can get a taxi or board the regular train for Torquay and its delights.

Scenes from Childhood

In one of the most charming passages in her autobiography, Christie recalls first attending church. Because the memory involves her father, who loved the service but died when she was 11, it has particular poignancy. The parishioners of the small church in Tor Mohun, the original hamlet that became Torquay, decided they needed a larger church. Agatha's father made a donation in her name shortly after her birth. When she was told this made her a founder of All Saints Torre, she repeatedly asked when she could go to church. At last the big day came.

The servants dutifully dropped the family off at the large church while they went on to the old smaller one, two streets away; with the other parishioners' servants, they would return after their shorter service just in time to take the gentry home. On that day, "Nursie" stood at the rear of the church in case Agatha wished to leave before the sermon. Agatha and her father sat in a pew near the front. Following the service in his big prayer book, she enjoyed herself so much that she shook her head when he offered to let her go. "Then," she says, "he took my hand in his and I sat contentedly, trying hard not to fidget." This initial visit to All Saints and those on successive Sundays marked the beginning of her lifelong attachment to churches.

Attending a service at All Saints makes it easy to see why young Agatha found church-going so attractive. The services are very high, with a sung Mass, solemn evensong, much incense and lots to watch without having to turn around: The celebrant, acolytes and deacons are at the altar, with the choir and organist positioned next to it. Just outside the communion rail is a shrine to Our Lady of Walsingham, Norfolk, with banks of vigil lights and a statue with a lace veil. The church has banners, a number of statues, side altars and the fourteen Stations of the Cross lining the walls. The baptismal font, moved from the old church of Agatha's christening, occupies a prominent place at the foot of the center aisle just inside the entrance. All Saints Torre, though designed in the style of Truro Cathedral by Pearson, is a comfortable, attractive church.

The way to the church appears unpromising: tourist hotels with garish flowers and surf boards in the front gardens line Belgrave Road as it comes up from the harbor. But, despite inevitable modern touches, after a left turn into Bampfylde Road, the old village of Tor Mohun emerges: old pillar boxes for the post, bright red call boxes, the upper floors of buildings unaltered, as attested by a sign in a window above a shut-up shop advertising a corsetiere who makes house calls. A right turn at the Bull and Rose pub to Elfrides Road where it joins Tor Church Road takes you to St. Xavier's Church. Agatha was baptized here and this is also the spot where she stood as proxy godmother for her sister Madge's son. St. Xavier's closed when the servant class disappeared between the wars and the parish had no need for two churches. Though it is now let to a Greek Orthodox congregation, its graveyard remains. White crosses, commemorating those who died in the two world wars, tell touching stories: "Lost at sea ... buried in Cairo ... buried at sea."

All Saints Vicarage at 45 Barton Road lies north and slightly west of the churches. Farther along Barton Road was Ashfield, the Miller house where Agatha spent her happy childhood. Open fields began just beyond the property when she was a child. But by 1938 the area had changed radically. The large villas had become boarding houses and nursing homes; some had been demolished. According to Janet Morgan, her official biographer, with her parents gone and now happily married to Max, Agatha felt she was free to leave Ashfield behind. She did not revisit the site for over 25 years, knowing it would cause her much pain. When she did she found that nothing remained—not a stick, not a blade of grass. Yet, she says in the epilogue to her autobiography, when she dreamed of a house, it was always Ashfield, "the house where I was born." Fortunately for today's visitor, at least one important remnant of her early years, All Saints Torre, still stands.

Torquay Tributes: A Room and a Statue
The Agatha Christie Room at Torre Abbey

Finding the Agatha Christie room in 12th-century Torre Abbey feels rather like solving an Agatha Christie mystery. The circuitous route winds through galleries, down corridors, and up a narrow staircase. Like the red herrings in Christie's novels, the museum's superb collection of ceramics, landscapes, portraits and furniture distracts the visitor.

The room is an inspired choice to house her memorial exhibit. A ghost and a headless monk reputedly walk nearby. Inside, in a medieval tower, an unseen clock ticks away; on the hour, accompanied by much creaking and grinding, its chimes shatter the silence in the former study of a prominent Torquay resident, the late Colonel Cary. The circular staircase which once connected the room to the tower, now lies inaccessible, behind the oak paneling installed over stone walls in 1906. The room, a dead-end, could inspire one of Agatha Christie's locked-room mysteries.

Agatha Christie's famous 1937 Remington portable typewriter, the only object in the room not behind glass, sits on a plain table against the far wall. Even in its traveling case, it looks ready for use because of its raised lid. With a quick snap to secure the top and a journey on the Orient Express, the typewriter could end up on another plain table at one of her husband's digs in the desert.

One massive purpose-built display case flanking the typewriter table contains editions of a number of her books, including the novels she wrote as Mary Westmacott. The handwritten manuscript of *A Caribbean Mystery* lies open, ready for comparison to the heavily edited draft (typed on the trusty Remington), and to the published edition. On a shelf in the bookcase above, Edgar Allan Poe, inventor of the mystery story, peers mournfully from the rows of memorabilia and photos connected with the publication of Christie's works; the Mystery Writers Association presented the ceramic bust, its Edgar, when it named Agatha a Grand Master in 1954. Across the room from the typewriter, editions of all her works take up the entire wall. In a corner cabinet hangs the academic robe worn while receiving an Honorary Doctor of Literature at Devon's University of Exeter, an especially significant honor since, like many of her social class in that period, she never attended school except for a short stint at a finishing school abroad.

Two prominent portraits—one a pastel by Oliver Snell hanging above the typewriter, and the other an oil by H. J. Baird hanging above the stone fireplace—bear little resemblance to each other or to exhibited photos of Agatha. The seemingly random objects in the case on the typewriter's left tantalize with hints of a real person. For example, in the last Miss Marple case, *Sleeping Murder*, Mrs. Mountford's back parlor is described:

> There was a picture made with shells and a watercolor of a very green sea at Capri. There were a great many other things, none of them with any pretensions to beauty or the higher life; but the net result was a happy cheerful room where people sat round and enjoyed themselves whenever there was time to do so.

Perhaps Agatha was describing the ambiance a visitor found in her own houses. The objects in the case look as if they were gathered by a very nice, quite ordinary woman who wanted to create a happy, cheerful room for herself and her family.

Though none of the memorabilia is labeled, her autobiography hints at the choices her family made about the room at Torre Abbey. Two framed embroideries and embroidered hand-held Victorian fire screens pay homage to two creative needlewomen—Agatha and her Grannie B. Agatha was very proud of her embroidery, learned at Abney from Grannie B, a master at landscapes and figures, particularly on fire screens. Agatha claims she never attained Grannie B's artistry; instead she traced flowers from Dresden vases and embroidered them on sofa cushions. Several porcelain figurines acknowledge another inherited passion: collecting china. Other collectibles—a boxed sewing kit, Tunbridge Ware papier-mâché boxes inlaid with mother-of-pearl, fans, inlaid wood boxes of the sort one finds in Spain—would have added to the comfortable atmosphere of the rooms Agatha enjoyed decorating in her various houses. And, as in Mrs. Mountford's back parlor, a framed round picture made of shells hangs on the wall beside the door. It can have only sentimental value. Where did the shells come from? Did she make the picture or did Rosalind or her grandson Mathew? This picture is composed of the odd delights one picks up as a child: as Christie put it, these are all "true treasures of life that one enjoys better than topazes, emeralds or expensive little boxes by Fabergé."

The Agatha Christie Bronze

The second of Torquay's two public tributes to its most famous native is a larger-than-life-sized bust that stands outside the Pavilion in Princess Gardens. The statue, on Cary

Parade, faces Fleet Street—locales Agatha Christie never mentions. More appropriately, the bust should face the Edwardian-style Pavilion that appeared in *The ABC Murders*. Alternatively, it could stand in another section of the Princess Gardens mentioned in the book, the shelter that faces Torquay harbor (a vista Christie herself enjoyed, especially when roller skating in her late teens on Princess Pier).

A Dutch sculptor and long-time Christie fan, Carol van den Boom-Cairns chose to develop the bust using photographs of a 50-year-old Agatha because, the sculptor said, "faces don't come to life until then." She noted that Christie had an intriguing face that revealed little. The statue shows a pleasant, middle-aged Agatha Christie: hair pinned up, clad in a dinner dress, the neckline graced with a single strand of pearls. The artist unveiled the statue at Cary Green in September 1990 as part of the Agatha Christie Centenary.

Public Places

Since Torquay and its environs meant so much to Agatha, she makes many references to the area in her works. She may have altered a name but her description makes it easily recognizable. For instance, *Peril at End House* is set at St. Loo, a seaside vacation spot much like Torquay. The plot hinges on efforts to preserve a family house; Agatha held on to Ashfield as long as possible and carefully protected Greenway House for her daughter, Rosalind. In *Ordeal by Innocence*, Dartmouth becomes Drymouth, lying seven miles along a spectacular coastal road from Redquay. To reach Sunny Point requires a short ferry ride across the Rubicon River, just as reaching Kingswear requires a ferry ride across the Dart. *Dead Man's Folly* is set at Nasse House, but Max suggested in his memoirs that its description marks it as Greenway, down to familiar identifiable landmarks in the garden.

Torquay's superb beaches inspired Agatha's lifelong love of swimming in the sea. She swam at Anstey Cove where every possible amenity for a pleasurable outing could be procured: picnic hampers; fresh crabs, lobsters and fish; pleasure boats; fishing tackle; swimming lessons. Bathing machines to protect ladies' modesty were available there well into the '20s. Women undressed in the little house on wheels, a horse in shafts pulled the machine out beyond the shallow water where it was deep enough to swim, and ladies dove out the open door facing away from the shore while the attendant looked discreetly away.

Torquay's sea front boasts other attractions. The glass Pavilion sits jewel-like in the center of the curve around the harbor. Formerly, it served as the focus for much of Torquay's activities. Today it has shops on the ground floor; at the top of the wide stair case, a comfortable restaurant encircles the atrium. The Princess Gardens features palm trees and sub-tropical plants. The harbor itself is crowded with fishing boats, sailboats, and yachts.

Torquay has over a hundred hotels. Apparently one of them served as the model for the television parody *Fawlty Towers*. Since no one knows which one, various proprietors claim bragging rights. Those who want to allow more time for exploring Torquay can easily find accommodation in their preferred price category. But they would do well to see a room beforehand, lest they hit upon the *Fawlty Towers*. prototype.

Three hotels that have Christie connections—The Grand, the Osbourne and the Imperial—bear no resemblance to the infamous Fawlty Towers. All front onto beaches, offering patrons superb views. The Grand Hotel, 100 yards from the station, overlooks Corbyn Sands with views across Torbay toward the Marina and Pavilion. There Agatha and Archie spent their wedding night—Christmas Eve, 1914—but the view was surely lost on them. They arrived at midnight after a horrendous train journey from Archie's home at Clifton. They had spent the previous three days procuring the license that allowed them to marry before Archie shipped out to France with The Royal Flying Corps. On Boxing Day, December 26, they were again on a train—to London—where they began a six-month enforced separation. Though today the Grand features leisure breaks, attendees at business conferences would be more likely to choose it than honeymooners. The white Edwardian building with regatta blue exterior fire escapes and trim makes an arresting sight. The location across from the Torquay station, as well its high standard of comfort and food, makes the four-star hotel a popular choice.

The five crown Osbourne Hotel occupies a magnificent Regency Crescent. Called the Royal Clarence in *The Sleeping Murder*, it is the oldest hotel in town. Christie describes its mellow bowfronted facade, adding that it catered to the type of family who came for a month at the seaside. The Osbourne, with over five acres of private gardens for walking and Meadfoot Beach for swimming, appeals to families and others who enjoy an old-world atmosphere.

The Imperial, sitting high on a cliff overlooking Torbay, is Torquay's most luxurious hotel. Most of the 150 bedrooms and 17 suites have a seaview and private balcony. In the evening, jacket and tie are required in the magnificent Regatta restaurant, famous for its "Gastronomic Weekends," as well as in the ballroom where guests can dance to live music after dinner. The hotel has extensive sports facilities, but those in search of exercise will do better to take advantage of walks through the hotel's subtropical gardens, across its lawns and along its winding terraced pathways. Or best of all, they could swim at Christie's favorite bathing place—nearby Beacon Cove.

The Imperial offers travelers a chance to end their journey where Miss Marple ended hers. Christie wrote *The Sleeping Murder* during World War II but secured it in a vault with orders that it was not to be published until after her death. When it came time for her readers to see Miss Marple for the last time, Agatha Christie knew exactly where she should be: sitting at a table on the Sun Terrace at the Imperial, unraveling the mystery so that the young husband and wife, Giles and Gwenda, can live happily ever after in the house of their dreams, Hillside House. Today there could be no more satisfying way to end this journey than to spend the end of a golden summer afternoon on the Imperial's terrace with its view of Christie's beloved Torbay. Order a cream tea, ignore the tea, and help yourself to Agatha's favorite, Devonshire cream.

Return to London: train from Torquay straight through to Paddington.

Christie Works Mentioned in This Chapter

Evil Under the Sun
The Hollow
Dead Man's Folly
"The Regatta Mystery" in *The Regatta Mystery, Poirot Lends a Hand, Thirteen for Luck*
An Autobiography
A Caribbean Mystery
Sleeping Murder
The ABC Murders

Peril at End House
Ordeal by Innocence

Contacts and Resources for This Chapter

Totnes Tourist Information Centre, The Plains, Totnes TQ9 5EJ. Telephone: (01803) 863-168.

Dart Pleasure Craft, River Link. Telephone: (01803) 834-488.

Torbay and Dartmouth Steam Railway, Queens Park Station, Paignton TQ4 6AF. Telephone: (01803) 555-872. Open Easter, then end of May to early October 10 a.m. to 4 p.m. daily. Santa specials in December.

The English Riviera Tourist Board, The Tourist Centre, Vaughan Parade Torquay TQ2 5JG. Telephone: (01803) 297-428; Fax: (01803) 214-885.

The Imperial Hotel, Park Hill Rd., Torquay TQ1 2DG. Telephone: (01803) 294-301, or in the United States 1-800-225-5843.

The Grand Hotel, Torbay Rd. Torquay TQ2 6NT. Telephone: (01803) 296-677.

Osbourne Hotel, Hesketh Crescent, Torquay TQ1 2LL. Telephone: (01803) 213-311.

Moorland Hotel, Haytor, Dartmoor, Newton Abbot TQ13 9XT. Telephone: (01364) 661-407.

Torre Abbey, The Kings Drive, Torquay TQ2 5JX. Telephone: (01803) 293-593. Open April through October daily 9:30 a.m. to 6 p.m.; November through March, parties only by appointment.

Torquay Museum, 529 Babbacombe Rd., Torquay TQ1 1HG. Telephone: (01803) 293-975. Open Easter through October: Monday through Saturday 10 a.m. to 4:45 p.m.; Sunday 1:30 p.m. to 4:45 p.m. November to Easter: Monday through Friday 10 a.m. to 4:45 p.m.

Kents Cavern, Ilsham Rd., Torquay TQ1 2JF. Telephone: (01803) 294-059. Open daily 10 a.m. to varied closing (5 p.m. to 9 p.m.) depending on season.

Cockington Country Park, Torquay TQ2 6XA. Telephone: (01803) 690-495.

Dartmouth Tourist Information Centre, The Engine House, Mayor's Avenue, Dartmouth TQ6 9YY. Telephone: (01803) 834-224.

Salcombe Tourist Information Centre, Council Hall, Market St., Salcombe TQ8 8DE. Telephone: (01548) 843-927.

All Saints Torre, Bampfylde Road, Torquay. All Saints Vicarage, 45 Barton Rd., Torquay TQ1 4DT. Telephone: (01803) 326-692. Mass daily. Sunday evensong.

10

Agatha and Apples

APPLES PLAYED A ROLE in one of the most romantic inter-ludes in Christie's first marriage. In 1916 during Archie's second leave, they took a walk through an orchard on the path to Nomansland, a village at the northern edge of the New Forest in Hampshire. A woman there gave them permission to eat all the apples they wanted. "You're welcome to the apples. Your man is in the air force, I see—so was a son of mine who was killed. Yes, you go and help yourselves to all the apples you can eat." And so they did, happily munching, not even minding the gentle rain that fell as they sat under the trees in the most ancient of English woodlands, set aside nine centuries ago by William the Conqueror as his "new" hunting forest.

Agatha loved apples and lamented her fate when she could no longer chew them because of problems with her teeth. Poirot's sometime side-kick, Ariadne Oliver, loves apples. She has Christie's penchant for eating them in the bath. In Mrs. Oliver's very first appearance in one of the Parker Pyne stories, she has a bag of apples beside her desk, as essential to writing her detective stories as a typewriter. To Poirot's consternation, Mrs. Oliver keeps an untidy house with apple cores and papers strewn all about. In *Dead Man's Folly,* when she rises to meet Poirot, several apples fall from her lap and roll in all directions. Most distressing of all is an incident in *Mrs. McGinty's Dead*, when an apple core tossed from an open car window hits Poirot smartly on the cheek. He knows its source at once though he has no inkling Mrs. Oliver is in the area. Indeed, as she emerges from her car, Cox apples dropping from the capacious folds of her clothing roll down the hill.

The apples for which Agatha and her fictional counterpart, Ariadne Oliver, had such affection bear no resemblance to the ubiquitous Delicious and Granny Smiths of today with their smooth skins, even color and bland flavor. The apples she enjoyed bear names such as Annie Elizabeth, Beauty of Bath, Orleans Reinette, Merton Knave, Tydeman's Late Orange. These apples can still be found, although it takes some doing. Many of these older varieties need to be handled and packed with care and don't adapt to the discipline of the supermarket.

A journey along a country road like that taken by Agatha and Archie in 1916 can bring rewards: Many a farmer displays freshly picked apples at the farm entrance, and customers leave the money in the honesty box. Some things never change, at least in Agatha Christie country.

Christie Works Mentioned in This Chapter

"The Case of the Discontented Soldier" in *Parker Pyne Investigates/Mr. Parker Pyne, Detective*
Dead Man's Folly
Mrs. McGinty's Dead

Contacts and Resources for This Chapter

New Forest Tourist Information Centre, High Street, Lynd-hurst, Hampshire, SO43 7NY. Telephone: (01703) 282-269. Open all year.

Fordingbridge Tourist Information Centre, the nearest to Nomansland. Telephone: (01425) 654-560. Seasonal Open-ing—Easter to mid-September.

11

Murder Abroad

SINCE SHE LOVED to travel all her life, it is not surprising that Christie set some of her books in countries other than England. She and her first husband, Archie Christie, went around the world after the First World War on a Trade Commission under the direction of an acquaintance from Archie's school days, Major Belcher. In memory of that journey, she wrote *The Man in the Brown Suit*, a thriller set on shipboard and in South Africa. It features the first appearance of Colonel Race along with a heroine whose late father was an expert on Neanderthal man. In 1989, CBS used a contemporary setting when adapting it for television.

After her divorce in 1928, Agatha, fascinated by archaeology, went alone on her first visit to the Middle East. On her second trip, she met her archaeologist husband-to-be, Sir Max Mallowan. During their 46-year marriage, she accompanied him on numerous digs, helping with excavations during the day and composing mystery novels on her trusty Remington typewriter in the evening. The locale figured in several of her books. In *Murder in Mesopotamia*, Poirot is on a dig along the Tigris River in Iraq. As part of vacation in Jerusalem, he takes a side trip to a desert city where an officious stepmother keeps an *Appointment with Death*. The 1988 feature film starred Peter Ustinov as Poirot.

Drawing on her familiarity with Baghdad where she and Max maintained a house for many years, Agatha created a 1951 novel of political intrigue and espionage focusing on a secret pact between the Big Three powers—Britain, Russia and the United States—when *They Came to Baghdad.*

Christie wrote two books set in Egypt, 4,000 years apart. *Death on the Nile* takes place in the '30s. The 1978 film, with Ustinov as Poirot, captures the glamour of that period. The other marked a departure for Christie, who focused on settings roughly contemporaneous with the pyramids' construction. Set in the Nile Valley in 2000 B.C., *Death Comes as an End* focuses on murders that occur in the family of a wealthy priest-landowner in ancient Thebes.

Another novel, set on the western coast of North Africa, is based on a real espionage case about two physicists who betrayed their countries to become Russian spies. The thriller, *Destination Unknown/So Many Steps to Death,* is set in exotic Casablanca in the '50s. An equally exotic but more benign locale finds Miss Marple involved in *A Caribbean Mystery* on her only sleuthing venture outside Britain. In filmed versions, two fine actresses play Miss Marple: Helen Hayes starred in the Warner Brothers film in 1983 and Joan Hickson in the 1989 BBC production.

Planes and trains gave Christie the opportunity to work variations on the sealed room formula. In *Death in the Clouds/Death in the Air*, written in 1935, the murder takes place aboard the *Prometheus* on a flight from Paris to London. Poirot works with Scotland Yard and the Sûretè, with the latter doing superior work. In 1992, London Weekend News mounted a version also shown in the United States on

PBS. Christie's frequent trips to the Middle East inspired what is arguably her most popular mystery, especially after the superb 1974 film with an all-star cast and Albert Finney as Poirot. *Murder on the Orient Express/Murder in the Calais Coach* occurs when the famous train is halted by a snowstorm in Yugoslavia on its way west from the Middle East. Le Train Bleu, a train even more elegant than the Orient Express, carries Poirot and a group of exceedingly wealthy passengers to winter on the French Riviera in *The Mystery of the Blue Train*. This is the novel Christie claimed never should have been written; it is far below her usual standard.

France is the setting for another Poirot novel—*Murder on the Links*. However, the game of golf plays no role in the plot save for the fact that the murder victim is buried in a shallow grave on the course adjoining his villa. In this novel Hastings falls in love with his future wife who is one of the suspects. Christie set her last espionage novel on the continent. The action in *Passenger to Frankfurt* occurs mainly in Germany. The novel is her reaction to the '60s, drugs, the threat of a new Aryan superman and a vaguely defined "Third World."

Two non-mystery novels Christie published under the pseudonym of Mary Westmacott take place outside the United Kingdom. *Unfinished Portrait*, set on a Spanish island where an artist saves a young woman from suicide, is a blend of autobiography and imagination, according to Max. *Absent in Spring* brings Christie back to Mesopotamia, this time as an opportunity for the heroine to examine her life when isolated from family and friends.

Christie's books set in non-English settings are some of her best. Today it is possible to travel to Christie crime scenes far beyond the English Channel. Those who take the journey won't be disappointed.

Christie Works Mentioned in This Chapter

The Man in the Brown Suit
Murder in Mesopotamia
Appointment with Death
They Came to Baghdad
Death on the Nile
Death Comes as an End
Destination Unknown/So Many Steps to Death
A Caribbean Mystery
Death in the Clouds/Death in the Air
Murder on the Orient Express/Murder on the Calais Coach
Mystery of the Blue Train
Passenger to Frankfurt

And writing as Mary Westmacott:
Unfinished Portrait
Absent in Spring

12

Parapsychology

WHEN CONFRONTED WITH a series of seemingly unrelated deaths on a dig at an Egyptian tomb, Poirot wisely remarks, "You must not underrate the force of superstition." His warning proves correct when he shows that, to cover his crimes, a murderer has depended upon a widely held belief in a death curse on those who enter the tomb.

Agatha Christie understood well the public fascination with matters not strictly explainable by logic and science. She herself had experienced something of the kind, as she relates in *An Autobiography*:

> *It was going up in the train to Manchester that I knew, quite suddenly, that my mother was dead. I felt a coldness, as though I was invaded all over, from head to feet with some deadly chill and I thought: 'Mother is dead.'*

She plays upon a premonition of disaster in the short story "The Red Signal." The hero, who can sense danger when it is near, makes a nearly fatal misreading of its source, though he is not taken in by a seance.

Christie, however, *does* expect her readers to be taken in

by parapsychology, using it as a distraction from straight mystery and detection. She does it most effectively in *The Sittaford Mystery/Murder at Hazelmoor,* which opens with a seance during a snowstorm in a remote Dartmoor village, a perfect cover for a murderer. She capitalizes on a veritable craze for pseudo-scientific paraphernalia, which began in the late 19th century and peaked in England during the 1950s. Poirot acknowledges that he always interests himself in matters of the occult, implying that he knows how cleverly such devices can be used to deceive.

The planchette, invented in 1853 by a well-known French spiritualist, became a mania in America and Great Britain after a firm of American toy makers manufactured copies and marketed them in book shops. The very simple instrument, of which the Ouija board is a variation, consists of a thin heart-shaped piece of wood mounted on a tripod of two small casters and a pencil. A spirit presumably operates through the psychic force of the medium who places a hand on the wood, causing the pencil to produce automatic writing.

Influenced by Madame Helena Blavatsky, the founder of the Theosophical Movement, writers such as the Nobel prize-winning poet, William Butler Yeats, published works based upon the results of automatic writing. Though The Society for Psychical Research exposed such fraudulent claims, the planchette and its various forms remained popular throughout Christie's lifetime. One of her beaus, Wilfred Pirie, became interested in spiritualism and she dutifully read the books but found them "tedious ... completely false ... nonsense." She describes her feelings when she broke off with him: "Oh joy, oh joy, I would not have to read any more theosophy." But she later used that knowledge in her books.

The Black Box, a more complicated instrument than the planchette, serves as a clever plot device in one of Christie's own favorite novels, *The Pale Horse*. She realized that the device, believed to cure disease, also may cause harm since it can be used on patients without their knowledge.

The inventor of the Black Box, an unconventional San Francisco physician, Albert Abrams, claimed diagnosis and cure of ailments in patients from any distance. Originally, the device consisted of a box called the E. R. A. or Oscilloclast, with rheostats and a thin sheet of rubber mounted over a metal plate. The patient's blood sample was put into the machine, which was connected to a metal plate on the forehead of a healthy person; by tapping that person's abdomen and stroking the rubber sheet, the doctor determined the patient's disease, the diagnosis depending on the psychic connection between the patient and his blood sample.

Later versions of the Box, introduced long after Abrams' death in 1924, feature colored liquids, rows of knobs to twirl and legitimate sounding terms such as electromagnetic fields, chabras, L-fields, T-fields, emanations. Instead of blood, the patient's hair could be used. In *The Pale Horse*, Thyrza Grey needs only some personal object, in this case a glove, to insert into the Box in order to find "a weak spot ... deep in the tissues of the flesh" and thus lead the absent victim "towards death—the true way, the natural way" by natural causes. Mark Easterbrook, the desperate narrator of the novel, thinks the box represented the development of scientific possibility. Christie knows that the reader, like Easterbrook, will find it hard to discount the Box. It serves her purpose of providing cover for the real method of murder.

The Pale Horse and *The Sittaford Mystery/Murder at Hazelmoor* show her obvious skepticism about the physical trappings connected with the occult. But Agatha's stories, most notably those collected in *The Hound of Death*, reveal the influence of her early experience with e.s.p. following her mother's death. Slightly ahead of her time, Christie realized correctly that this fascination with the paranormal would doubtless add to the timeless quality of her books, eagerly embraced by new generations.

Christie Works Mentioned in This Chapter

"The Adventure of the Egyptian Tomb" in *Poirot Investigates*

An Autobiography

"The Red Signal" in *The Hound of Death*

The Sittaford Mystery/Murder at Hazelmoor

The Pale Horse

13

Wallingford

A DAY OUT IN Wallingford makes clear why Agatha Christie spent more time there than any other place. The Mallowans purchased Winterbrook House in 1934 and lived there off and on until their deaths, hers in January 1976, his one and a half years later. Both are buried in nearby St. Mary's Churchyard.

Wallingford is a charming, medieval market town somewhat off the beaten path and treasured by Agatha for its privacy and seclusion from the limelight. Indeed, virtually nothing of Agatha's life at Winterbrook appears in her books. Even in the '30s Wallingford had poor railway service; the late '50s saw its last regularly scheduled train. It was never the sort of place people "came to." Wallingford is a real find for the Christie fan and anyone else who would enjoy visiting a small but thriving typical English market town.

When Agatha and Max bought Winterbrook House, Max said that he thought they were going to be very happy there. And sure enough, they were, as Agatha wrote 35 years later in her autobiography. Wallingford proved just the right spot for the country house they needed for weekends away from their work in London. Four years into their marriage, she

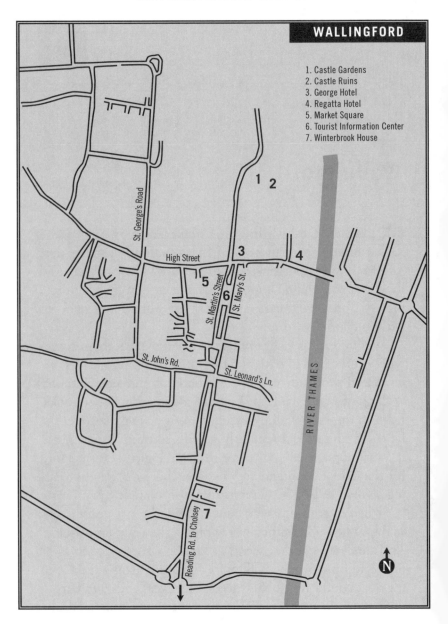

WALLINGFORD

1. Castle Gardens
2. Castle Ruins
3. George Hotel
4. Regatta Hotel
5. Market Square
6. Tourist Information Center
7. Winterbrook House

and Max were successful writers, he an expert on the archae-ology of the ancient Near East, she the author of over a dozen detective novels. The five-hour trip to Torquay had become too time consuming.

Initially, they looked for a simple cottage somewhere along the Thames: Max loved the river and knew the countryside well, having spent some of the happiest years of his life at Oxford. Their search up and down the Thames proved fruit-less; they found either hideous Victorian houses or cottages that were under water in winter. But Agatha, with her nose for property, saw an advertisement for—not a cottage—but a five-bedroom house just outside Wallingford. They snatched up the small Queen Anne on their first visit and promptly left for nine months on a dig in Syria.

Agatha always said that Winterbrook was Max's house and, indeed, he found the house congenial to his personal-ity. It had good proportions and gracious windows, over-looking a feature he valued, water meadows down to the river. He had a whole floor with river views for his library. Wallingford offered quick access to London and even quicker access to Oxford where he kept up his contacts at New Col-lege and at All Souls, where he taught beginning in the '60s. Through the years, the Mallowans divided their time between various London residences and Wallingford, with trips to Torquay for Rosalind's school holidays and for post-World War II summers when Greenway House was derequisitioned by the American forces.

Agatha herself liked the house. She immediately saw the potential for increasing the size of the lawn by expanding into the water meadow, creating a perfect setting for tea under a fine cedar tree. She cultivated a garden, with special attention to her white peonies. A covered squash court was built, later serving as temporary storage for the furniture salvaged from their bombed London residence on Sheffield Terrace. The Thames offered plenty of wonderful spots for the picnics Agatha loved and ample opportunity for watching people messing about in boats, particularly at the nearby Marina and at the Wallingford and Henley Regattas. Except for summers in Torquay and forays into London, Agatha spent the last 10 years of her life at Winterbrook. Near the end, her bed was moved downstairs and Max continued his writing sitting beside her. She died one January day just after luncheon, Max at her side at Winterbrook.

Wallingford's appeal becomes apparent on a day trip from London, particularly since it can easily include a visit to Oxford for tea and a look around Max's colleges. Trains departing Paddington twice an hour reach Cholsey, the nearest station, in just over an hour. Like the residents of St. Mary Mead who had to phone a local taxi for the two mile trip from Much Benham, today's visitor can do the same for Wallingford, ringing the number posted above the phone outside the station. A bus runs every hour to Wallingford or the walk into town is pleasant if the weather is fine.

Winterbrook House stands close to the Reading Road on the way into Wallingford from Cholsey. It lies on the right side of the road just beyond Winterbrook Lane opposite. The house is privately owned and cannot be visited. But the Thames Footpath runs beside it and along the water meadow below the garden, allowing a view of the squash court (now converted into living quarters) and the house itself. When Winterbrook came up for sale, the Wallingford Town Council voted not to purchase it, a decision much bemoaned by many of the town's 10,000 residents, particularly the volunteers at the Tourist Information Centre located in the Town Hall.

Wallingford offers much to see and do. The Market Place is especially bustling on Friday—Market Day—when everything from fresh flowers and produce to housewares is ranged round the Market Cross. The shops draw a steady stream of customers. Toby English Books and Prints stocks children's books by many of the authors Christie remembers reading. Refreshment can be found in the attractive tea shops and cafes. The Coach and Horses, noted locally for its excellent beer and good food, is on the Kinecroft, a mound marking the ancient ramparts that defended the town under the Romans, Saxons and Normans. The George Hotel is one of the charming old inns located on the quaint streets of Wallingford. Dick Turpin, the highwayman, is reputed to have stayed there. Now part of the Mt. Charlotte Thistle chain, the George has a fine restaurant and offers attractive weekend packages. The Regatta Hotel, with its Thames-side setting, makes a good spot to quaff a draft while watching activity on the river.

A stroll through the Castle Gardens makes for a pleasant interlude. In 1993, they were declared the Best Park, Central Southern England in Bloom. They are all that remains of what was one of the strongest and most important castles in England. In 1154, Henry II held his first Parliament there and subsequently gave the town its first charter. But the Black Death caused royalty to abandon Wallingford in the 14th century; stones from the castle were used for repairs to Windsor Castle in the 16th century; and Cromwell ordered the castle demolished for his revenge on Wallingford as the last stronghold of royalist support in the 17th century civil war. A few walls of the castle keep stand, along with the ruins of the tower and a 16th-century church, one of 15 that once stood in Wallingford.

Another attraction is the Cholsey and Wallingford Railway, the C&WR. Opened in 1866 and now run entirely by volunteers, it is one of the oldest surviving Great Western Railway Branch lines in the Thames Valley. Until its service ended, Agatha and Max would have used this steam railway to get to London and to Oxford, as well as to Reading for transfer to the Devon train. Today, thanks to the infamous Lord Beeching, there is no regular service but rides can be taken on some Sundays and holidays, April through September, and on Santa specials in December. Plans call for the line to run to Cholsey station.

Trains run from Cholsey to Oxford every half hour and the journey takes just 15 minutes. Arrival in Oxford before five would allow for a proper afternoon tea at the Randolph Hotel, in the room where C. S. Lewis and his Joy had their first tea in *Shadowlands* and where Inspector Morse has been known to take his tea on the rare occasions when he isn't having a pint in a pub. Alternatively, a walk round Oxford would allow a visit to Max's college, New College, founded in 1379, on New College Lane off Queen's Lane. It can be entered Easter through September, daily from 11 a.m. to 5 p.m., and in winter from 2 p.m. to 5 p.m.

Max later lived at 6 Ship St. behind Jesus College. In 1962 he was made a fellow at All Souls College, located across Cattle Street from the Radcliffe Camera. Agatha and Max liked to entertain friends for dinner at All Souls.

Oxford has many excellent restaurants. With so much to see in the city of dreaming spires, the day could end well with dinner and a late train back to London.

The Mallowans are buried in Cholsey at St. Mary's, a little country church Agatha favored. Several magnificent yews guard the churchyard and at the rear stands the imposing white grave marker. Writ large are their names: Agatha Mary Clarissa Mallowan, DBE [Dame of the British Empire] and Max Edgar Lucien Mallowan, KT [Knight]. In smaller letters beneath are carved their respective professions: Agatha Christie, Author and Playwright; Max Mallowan, Archaeologist. In smaller letters yet is the quotation from Spenser's *Faerie Queene* that she requested:

> "*Sleepe after toyle, port, after stormie seas/Ease after war, death after life, does greatly please.*"

Train: Paddington to Cholsey; Cholsey to Oxford. Return: Oxford to Paddington.

Contacts and Resources for This Chapter

Wallingford Tourist Information Centre, 9 St. Martin's St. OX10 0AL. Telephone: (01491) 826-972. Fax: (01491) 826-550. Open Monday through Friday 9 a.m. to 1 p.m. & 2 p.m. to 5 p.m.; closes Friday 4:30 p.m.

The George Hotel, High St. OX10 0BS. Telephone: (01491) 836-665. Fax: (01491) 825-593. Thistle Hotels: in the United States 1-800-847-4358.

The Regatta Hotel, Wallingford Bridge OX10 0BL. Telephone: (01491) 826-126.

The Cholsey & Wallingford Railway Preservation Society. Hithercroft Road. Telephone: (0491) 835-067. Limited operation so phone for schedule.

Oxford Tourist Information Centre, The Old School, Gloucester Green. Telephone: (01865) 726-871. Monday through Saturday 9:30 a.m. to 5 p.m.; Sunday 10 a.m. to 3:30 p.m.

The Randolph Hotel, Beaumont St., OX1 2LN. Telephone: (01865) 247-481.

New College, New College Lane, off Queen's Lane. Telephone: (01865) 279-555. Easter to September daily 11:30 a.m. to 5 p.m.; during term 2–5 p.m.

All Souls College, High Street at Cattle St. Telephone: (01865) 279-379. Monday through Friday 2–4:30 p.m.

The Getaway Guide

14

Practicalities

Beware: Information changes very quickly. Area codes and phone numbers, opening and closing hours, addresses—all are subject to change. Before finalizing plans, be sure to check all information carefully. The best source of information is always the Tourist Information Centre in the city or town you visit.

Important Preliminary Steps: Once you make the decision to follow the Christie trail, contact the British Travel Authority (BTA) to request their Vacation Planner as well as their Accommodation Guides for Hotels, Bed and Breakfasts, and City Apartments. Respond to the ads the BTA and other official United Kingdom tourist organizations—such as the London Tourist Board—run in magazines and newspapers. By calling the toll free numbers, you will receive materials that would convince even a reluctant traveler to visit England. BTA has its main office at 551 Fifth Ave., New York, NY 10176-0799, open Monday through Friday 9 a.m. to 6 p.m. Phone 1-800-462-2748 or 212-986-2200. The BTA office in Chicago's Loop at 625 North Michigan Ave., Suite 1510, accepts walk-ins only, Monday through Friday from 9 a.m. to 5 p.m.

Even if time constraints prevent a visit to Torquay, you will want to read the tempting material provided free by the English Riviera Tourist Board. Write to the Tourist Centre, Vaughan Parade, Torquay TQ2 5JG; telephone: (01803) 296296. For $10 they also can send an excellent 52-page book on Christie's Devon, *Exploring Agatha Christie Country* by David Garrard.

Finally, you might want to treat yourself to membership in the Agatha Christie Society, P. O. Box 1896, Radio City Station, New York, NY 10101-1896. The $24 annual fee includes the quarterly *Christie Chronicle*.

Getting around: The length of your stay in the city, the Christie sites you would like to include, and the other places you wish to visit will determine how you best can get around once you arrive. Taxis are wonderful and relatively inexpensive. But you'll want to take advantage of London's effective public transportation system. For a week-long stay or sightseeing limited to London with at most a couple of short day-trips, your most economical and handiest choice is to purchase tickets for individual journeys at each Tube station. If you plan four or more journeys in a day, at Underground station ticket booths purchase Travelcards that allow travel on the Tube and London buses. However, the London Visitor Travelcard offered through BritRail that must be obtained before leaving the United States is no bargain: you would need to make seven trips per day on the Tube to break even and the restaurant vouchers and entry fee vouchers to London tourist attractions have nominal value. These pre-purchased cards also involve some inconvenience as they can be activated only at the airports or at one of two Tube stations— Victoria or Piccadilly Circus.

If you plan to stay longer than a week and do much travel outside London, consider a BritRail Pass. You must buy it before leaving the United States. You can choose between a Classic Pass allowing 4, 8, 15, 22 days or a month of consecutive-day travel or a Flexipass for travel on any 4, 8 or 15 days within a month. The latter is the most sensible choice unless you want to travel every day of your holiday. Travel agents are well-stocked with BritRail brochures or phone British Rail at 1-888-BRITRAIL for a copy. But consider carefully, as the same people who sell the pre-journey London Visitor Travelcard sell the BritRail pass. The average cost for each day of BritRail pass use is $60.00; but only long journeys cost that much, so you would probably save money by purchasing individual tickets in England. However, because a pass is convenient and you can travel anytime—even during peak hours—you may consider it worth the price. Because it is virtually impossible to determine fares using BritRail in the United States, you can phone (0345) 48-49-50 in the U.K. for accurate, specific information on schedules, fares, and reservations. The same rail journey planning number works flawlessly while you are in England: courteous, knowledgeable staff handle calls 24 hours a day.

Use the combination of train, bus, and taxi to get you around London and anywhere else in Christie country and get the bonus of feeling like a native.

Don't even *think* about driving a car in London. When you arrive, you'll understand why. However, a car would be handy for at least some of the travel outside London.

Money: Sales of traveler's checks have been flat and no wonder—armed with a credit card and your ATM card, you can get around nicely, thank you very much, and save on fees at the same time. Visa Gold is the most widely accepted, though MasterCard and American Express work many places. Check with your bank to be sure your PIN will work in the United Kingdom.

You'll need British currency on arrival to get from the airport into the city. You can purchase some at either your departure airport or when you arrive but save your nerves by ordering pounds through your bank before departure. True, there will be a service fee, but if you buy either $100 or 100 pounds, the $5 fee will not up the exchange rate much.

Lodging: London consistently ranks among the most expensive cities in the world for tourists. The U.S. government has on occasion allotted its employees there the highest per diem allowance for any city abroad. Finding suitable lodging without destroying a travel budget presents a real challenge. The sheer variety and number of accommodations in every part of the city spoil one for choice. Trying to choose from the dizzying number of guides to London and England only makes the task more daunting.

What to do

Begin by contacting your travel agent, who should have all sorts of brochures on hand. Airline schemes, which include airfare and a choice of accommodation in several price ranges, offer good value. Armed with the hotel list in your chosen price range, you can purchase guide books in a bookstore or visit a public library to make an informed choice. Be sure to consider proximity to an Underground station when choosing a hotel. Though London taxis are marvelous (the best in the world), visiting sights along the Christie trail is easier and more economical by Tube.

Don't limit yourself to the hotels connected with air packages. In addition to consulting reliable guide books such as those listed below, use the hotel ads in the British travel magazines available at your local newsstand or bookstore, particularly *In Britain*, the British Tourist Authority's publication for readers in North America; for a special half-off introductory subscription, phone 1-800-5211-7848. *British Heritage*, a magazine geared to North American Anglophiles, also has good information: phone 1-800-829-3340 for subscription information.

Booking directly with a hotel can yield good rates. It never hurts to ask for special deals, a corporate rate or special week-end rates. Even if a hotel does not have a toll-free number, the overseas call may well pay for itself in savings. When ringing (one never says calling or phoning in Britain) directly from the United States, allow for the time difference, ranging from five hours later than the East Coast to eight hours later for the West. Dial 011-44, then the number in the U.K. without the 0 preceding the area code. For example, if you would like to stay at the Jenkins Hotel in the room used to film Poirot investigating *The Adventure of the Italian Nobleman*, dial 011-44-171-387-2067 from outside the country instead of phoning (0171) 387-2067 as you would in the U.K.

I highly recommend a travel agent. They can often get a better rate than the listed (or rack) rate, particularly with chains familiar to Americans as well as with those exclusive to the United Kingdom. Calling the chain's toll free number in the U. S. to compare with your travel agent's price will ensure the most advantageous rate; the price will be quoted and probably guaranteed in dollars. However, bear in mind that many hotels supposedly connected with chains are privately owned and when contacted directly can offer rates not available through the chain.

Best Western: 1-800-528-1234

Comfort Inns: 1-800-221-2222

Forte/Le Meridien Hotels: 1-800-225-5843

Hilton Hotels: 1-800-445-8667

Holiday Inn: 1-800-465-4329

Radisson Edwardian Hotels: 1-800-333-3333

Sheraton Hotels: 1-800-325-3585

Thistle Hotels: 1-800-847-4358

Travelers Advantage, a travel service, often can arrange substantial discounts that more than cover the $59.95 annual membership fee. Call 1-800-548-1116.

Some London clubs, like the New Cavendish—originally founded for members of the Voluntary Aid Detachment which Christie joined in World War I—have reciprocity with clubs abroad but require letters of introduction from the member's parent club. The luxurious St. James's Club in Mayfair does offer temporary membership to non-members, and has a toll-free number in the U. S.: 1-800-877-0447.

Bed and breakfasts in London are another choice, and agencies featuring those economical accommodations advertise in the tourist publications. Guide books also offer recommendations. If private bathroom facilities are important to you, be sure to book an en-suite room. For true economy consider out-of-term university housing. King's College London has more than 2,000 dormitory rooms available during the summer for individuals and families; though some rooms are en-suite, most have wash basins with shared bath and shower facilities. Contact King's Campus Vacation Bureau at (0171) 928-3777, or write them at King's College London, 127 Stamford St., Waterloo, London SE1 9NQ

If you plan to stay a week or more in London, renting an

apartment may be the best choice. The cost per person will be lower, and the convenience of a fridge and a cooker can significantly reduce costs. Again, consult guide books and adverts in the tourist magazines in addition to the London Tourist Board's *Where to Stay In London*, and the British Tourist Authority's *Apartments in London*—free publications you can obtain on request from the BTA.

Tried and True in London

Lodging

Jenkins Hotel, 45 Cartwright Gardens, Russell Square, London WC1H 9EH. Telephone: (0171) 387-2067. Fax (0171) 383-3139. *Tube:* Russell Square, Euston, or King's Cross.

Travel Inn, 141 Euston Rd., London NW1 2AU. Telephone: (0171) 554-3400 or (01582) 41-43-41. Fax (0171) 554-3419. *Tube:* Euston.

Travel Inn, Belvedere Rd., London SW1 7PB. Telephone: (0171) 902-1600 or (01582) 41-43-41. Fax (0171) 902-1619. *Tube:* Embankment or Westmininster Bridge.

Hotel Concorde, 50 Great Cumberland Place, London W1H 7FD. Telephone: (0171) 402-6169. Fax (0171) 724-1184. Apartments also available. *Tube:* Marble Arch.

Durrants Hotel, George Street, London W1H 6BJ. Telephone: (0171) 935-8131. Fax (0171) 935-8231. Fax (0171) 487-3510. *Tube:* Bond Street.

Food

Fortnum and Mason, The Fountain, 1818 Piccadilly, W1. Telephone: (0171) 734-8040. Tea, ice cream and some hot dishes like Welsh rarebit. *Tube:* Piccadilly Circus.

Wren at St. James, 197 Piccadilly SW1. Telephone: (0171) 437-9419. No credit cards. Vegetarian. Great soups. *Tube:* Piccadilly Circus.

Royal Academy of Arts Restaurant, Piccadilly, W1. Telephone: (0171) 439-7438. *Tube:* Piccadilly Circus.

Museum Tavern, 49 Great Russell St., WC1. Telephone: (0171) 242-8987. Directly across from the British Museum. Reasonable and friendly. *Tube:* Tottenham Court Rd.

Red Lion Pub, 2 Duke of York St. off Jermyn St., SW1. Telephone: (0171) 930-2030. No credit cards. Great fish and chips on Saturday. *Tube:* Piccadilly Circus.

Sherlock Holmes Pub and Restaurant (upstairs) 10 Northumberland St., WC1. Telephone: (0171) 930-2644. A bobby recommended this one! *Tube:* Charing Cross or Embankment.

Cittie of Yorke, 22–23 High Holborn, WC1. Telephone: (0171) 242-7670. Barristers, judges, financial types. Great atmosphere. *Tube:* Holborn or Chancery Lane.

King's Head and Eight Bells, 50 Cheyne Walk, SW3. Telephone: (0170) 352-1820. *Tube:* Sloane Square.

Ye Olde Cheshire Cheese. Wine Office Court, 145 Fleet St., EC4. Telephone: (0171) 353-6170. An historical pub and three dining rooms. Very English food. *Tube:* St. Paul's.

Sofra Restaurant. Shepherd's Market, Mayfair. Telephone: (0171) 493-3220. *Tube:* Green Park.

Tea: Hyde Park Hotel, 66 Knightsbridge, SW1. Telephone: (0171) 235-2000. No Christie connections but Queen Mother Elizabeth took the princesses here for tea. Just steps from Harrods, this is my favorite place for tea in all of London. *Tube:* Knightsbridge.

Useful Publications: A Short List

A to Z London—familiarly known as the *A to Zed*—is absolutely indispensable; with a scale of 1:22,000, it indexes even the tiniest lanes; now available at most American bookstores, its handier spiral-bound version is available at every London news stand.

Cheap Sleeps in London and *Cheap Eats in London* by Sandra A. Gustafson—at least as cheap as London can get for adults; lots of insightful personal commentary.

Fodor's City Pack: London—a true pocket guide that also features full-size maps.

Frommer's England—The Complete Guide to London and the Countryside—if you buy only one guidebook, this is probably the best choice for all-around information; includes a city map.

London for Families by Larry and Michael Lain—also includes advice on airfare, apartments, the underground and more.

London Knopf Guides—A real gem though the new streamlined edition sacrificed in-depth treatment of historical London for portability; well worth looking into for a

sense of present-day London with some interesting suggestions for lodging, food, and entertainment.

Time Out (weekly)—at all London newsstands, *the* guide
to all that's going on in the city.

Some Advice: Besides buying them from your local bookstore, you can order travel books by mail from independent
booksellers. Two who specialize are Book Passage in Corte
Madera, CA, at 1-800-999-7909 and Easy Going Travel Shop
and Bookstore, 1385 Shattuck Ave., Berkeley, CA 1-510-843-
6725.

And because last year's guide will often serve just as well,
check with your library and at used book sales. No need to
bring entire guide books along; tear out or photocopy the
relevant sections and leave the rest at home.

Suggestions for a Seven-Day Trip: This becomes five days
because you lose a day in transit and must spend the last day
getting to the airport two or three hours in advance of your
late morning or early afternoon flight. However, much can
be done on the Christie trail. And if your traveling companion is not a keen fan, he or she will be suitably entertained as well.

If you land at Gatwick, the cost will prohibit your taking a taxi, but you may decide to justify the 40 pounds fare
if you arrive at Heathrow. However, public transportation
is good from either airport.

From Heathrow, choose the Underground, the Airbus or
the new Heathrow Express train, whichever will get you closest to your lodging. Hail a taxi once you get into the city if
your stop means a walk of three or more blocks—after an

exhausting flight you need to pamper yourself a little. From Gatwick, the BritRail Gatwick Express or the National Express coach will take you to always-bustling Victoria Station where you can follow the signs to the taxi rank for transport to your hotel.

Use the afternoon to ease into London—the crowds and the dense traffic moving in an unfamiliar direction are confusing. If your travel package included a guided bus tour of London, this is the day to take it. Stop at a news agent's for the latest *Time Out* with its list of what's on and opening and closing times. At the same time, purchase your *London A to Z* and a good London map. To help with orientation and all the information you didn't know you'd want before leaving, don't visit the always crowded London Tourist Board Information Centre at Victoria. Instead, try the more civilized British Travel Centre at 1 Regent St, open Monday to Friday 9 a.m. to 6:30 p.m., Saturday until 5 p.m. and Sunday 10 a.m. to 4 p.m.

Take a leisurely afternoon tea in one of the elegant spots so beloved by Christie and her characters. Because you need to stay awake until bedtime in London, consider an early evening stroll, picking up a light snack. You can devise a route of your own, but a real mood-setter could be one of the Original London Walks, such as Jack the Ripper Haunts, Classic Crimes and Murders, any of those with ghosts in the title, or a pub crawl (though every walk pauses at one pub or more where at least snacks are available). Your hotel may have a brochure; if not, ring (0171) 624-3978 to find out which walks are scheduled for the night as well as the designated Tube stop to meet your guide. No reservations are necessary; the cost is around 5 pounds; the guides are knowledgeable and entertaining, and you get a real feel for the way the city works in just two hours.

On two London days, after you get your bearings, visit a neighborhood with Christie associations. Chelsea has two Christie residences and much more besides—King's Road with chic shops and antique stores frequented by Sloane's Rangers; the beautiful Royal Hospital and Gardens where you will see retired Royal Service veterans in their distinctive 18th-century uniforms; a veritable hoard of blue plaque houses marking the residences of the famous and infamous who called Chelsea home from the 16th-century to the present; and a maze of charming streets. Mayfair/St. James boasts two former Christie residences, the most elegant shops in all of London as well as Boodles, the club where Agatha liked to dine. Piccadilly, which bisects the two areas, beckons toward its Circus with landmark attractions as well as a number of shops and watering holes treasured by Christie and her characters.

For a real escape from the bustle, explore the St. John's Wood area where Agatha lived when she and Archie first came up to London. After a meander along the Canal Footpath, with a stop-over for a lunch at Crockers Folly Pub (0171) 286-6608 and a visit to Lord's Cricket Ground (0171) 289-1611, try Jason's Trip, taking tea aboard one of the canal boats leaving Little Venice for a cruise on Regent's Canal to Campden Town Market and back. Ring (0171) 286-3428 for departure times. And, of course, one evening must include *The Mousetrap,* still running and still good entertainment after all these years at St. Martin's Theatre (0171) 836-1443.

Take at least one day trip beyond London. Though it makes for a long day, you could choose Harrogate, the scene of Agatha's still unexplained disappearance. A prototypical Victorian spa town, it has made the transition into this century while retaining its original charm. Its public gardens and ambiance are so seductive that James Herriott frequently went there when he needed a day away from all his creatures, great and small.

A day could just as profitably be spent in Wallingford, where for over 40 years Agatha and Max made Winterbrook House their major residence. And no wonder. Because the train from Paddington on its way to Oxford goes only as close as Cholsey, Wallingford lies just far enough off the beaten path to have offered Agatha the privacy she craved. It also gives today's visitor a glimpse of non-tourist England. Ideally situated for sailing regattas on the Thames, Wallingford has prize-winning gardens and castle ruins. Try to visit on Friday—Market Day—when the Market Square bustles. Either before or after making the two-mile journey by foot or taxi between Cholsey and Wallingford, venture a quarter mile down the road from the station to pay your respects at the Mallowan tomb in St. Mary's Churchyard. This day could easily include a visit to Oxford; every half hour a train makes the 15-minute journey between the two towns.

Of course the ultimate day trip for anyone, Christie fan or not, would be an excursion on the Orient Express leaving from Victoria Station for forays through the English countryside. The many choices include Murder on the Orient Express and Haunts of Agatha Christie. Reach them at 1-800-524-2420 in the U. S. or at (0171) 805-5100 in London.

This itinerary will satisfy the avid Christie fan and interest the casual traveler as well because it allows time and energy for so many other activities and sights.

Suggestions for a Two- or Three-Week Stay: Such a sojourn means making some decisions before setting out for England, and considering the suggestions in the getting around section at the beginning of this chapter. You can opt to buy your train tickets as you go or you can select an appropriate BritRail pass: for a two-week stay choose the Flexipass good for any 8 days travel in one month; for a three-week stay, the Flexipass good for any 15 days travel in one month. You can pair the pass with a London Visitor Travelcard or purchase one-day Travelcards in London as needed. Combining rail, bus and taxi will enable you to visit all the Christie sites and more outside London.

Alternatively, you can arrange to rent a car for the portion of your trip that you will spend outside London. Try to arrange a pick-up and drop-off outside London, perhaps at the airport. Oxford is another possibility: after your week in London, take the train to Oxford, see the city, drive to see Wallingford and travel the rest of the Christie trail. After your week or two on the road, drop your rental at Oxford and make the hour and a half coach trip to Heathrow for your return flight.

A week in London without day trips allows time for theater, museums and music. Besides attending a performance of *The Mousetrap*, emulate Christie, who was an avid theater-goer. She especially loved Shakespeare; she made frequent allusion to his works in her books and in titles such as *By the Pricking of My Thumbs* and *Taken at the Flood*. She named her daughter after his most charming heroine—Rosalind in *As You Like It*. Tickets for the blockbuster shows take some scrambling but tickets for most plays nearly always can be purchased at the theater box offices, sometimes at reduced prices just before curtain. The Ticket Booth in Leiscester Square offers half-price tickets (cash only with a small booking fee tacked on) between noon and 2 p.m. for matinees and 2:30 to 6:30 for evening performances on the day of the show, but the queue can be long and you have no choice of seating—they sell the most expensive seats first.

Visit the British Museum to have a look at its treasures including the artifacts Max Mallowan helped collect (with a little help from Agatha). The Imperial War Museum highlights not just the combatants in the two world wars but brings alive the conditions for those on the Home Front. Follow it up with a visit to the Christie Sheffield Terrace residence for a look at the rebuilding after the Blitz.

Art museums fit on the Christie trail. References to British painters such as Stubbs, Gainsborough, Sargent and Augustus Johns as well as to Velasquez, Dutch painters and moderns such as Gaugin and Miro dot the pages of Christie's books. London has plenty of places to see their works and those of others as well. The National Gallery, Royal Academy of Arts and the Tate have wonderful collections, beautifully displayed. The Courtauld's gorgeous paintings hang in a most uncongenial setting but are worth a visit nevertheless, especially if you follow up with drinks or tea at the Savoy just across the way.

If you attend a concert or the opera, you will follow closely in Agatha Christie's footsteps. She enjoyed music as the many references in her work make clear. She wanted to become a professional pianist until discovering public appearances paralyzed her. Nonetheless, she continued to play all her life. Christie particularly liked Bach and Elgar—at her direction, the Nimrod section of his *Enigma Variations* was played at her memorial service. Operetta pleased her—she fondly recalls performances of Gilbert and Sullivan and Fall's *The Rose of Stambul*. But her real love was opera, especially Wagner, the composer of her favorite *Der Rosenkavalier*.

On BritRail you can spend the next week or two visiting nearly all the Christie sites beyond London. Break your trip to Harrogate with a stop-over in York to visit the Minster with its breathtaking Five Sisters Window in the north transept. Walk the city wall and stroll through the Shambles. In Harrogate, you can stay at the hotel Agatha chose when she disappeared—the Old Swan, Swan Road, (01423) 500-055. Or book into the delightful, much less pricey Russell Hotel, Valley Drive, telephone: (01423) 509-866. It overlooks Valley Gardens and features a very nice restaurant and bar.

Spend two nights in Wallingford and include a Friday to see a Market Day in a typical English town. The George Hotel on the High Street is part of the Thistle chain. Phone the hotel directly for week-end specials at (01491) 836-665. Be sure to make time for a day trip to Oxford. Before catching one of the frequent trains for the 15-minute journey back to Cholsey/Wallingford, take tea at the Randolph Hotel where C. S. Lewis first met his Joy in *Shadowlands*.

Allow at least two full days and three nights for Torquay and environs, stopping off in Totnes on a Tuesday in summer when the townspeople don Elizabethan costume. For maximum Christie connections in Torquay, book into The Imperial Hotel by ringing (01803) 294-301 or find lodging following the staff's advice at The Tourist Centre, Vaughan Parade, (01803) 296-296. Torquay has many other attractions, including great beaches which Agatha enjoyed. The Torquay Natural History Museum also deserves a visit for its fascinating displays and a room devoted to the daughter of a member elected in 1894—Frederick Alvah Miller. Other delights are Cockington Village with thatched roof cottages and a working forge; and Kents Cavern where cave dwellers 30,000 years ago strewed animal bones among the stalactites and stalagmites. The English Riviera Tourist Board offers suggestions that will satisfy any visitor.

If you have used BritRail exclusively, you might like to gather courage at this point and rent a car for the duration of your stay in Devon. However, every place in the area is accessible by combining rail, bus and taxi. I prefer to travel like a local rather than a tourist on holiday and I have met such interesting people on public transportation. Take a day trip to Salcombe, a lovely yachting resort featured in *Towards Zero*. Picnic on Dartmoor as Christie loved to do all her life. Consider staying at the Moorland Hotel in Haytor as she did when completing her first novel—though fire later gutted the interior, the outside looks much as it did when she spent two weeks there in 1916; at least stop in for tea or for a drink in the Agatha Christie Bar, the hotel's homage to their most famous guest. The Art Deco Burgh Island Hotel at Bigbury-on-Sea makes a fine day trip. Take tea or drinks in the Palm Court or perhaps a pint in the nearby Pilchard Inn. But an overnight escape to the island hideaway, perhaps in the Christie suite with its separate sitting room and full length balcony, evokes the Golden Age of Detective Fiction as nothing else could.

Whatever your degree of familiarity with England, length of stay or means of transportation, the Christie trail promises a trip to remember for everyone in your party.

7 Days in London

Day 1: Arrive in London. Visit the British Travel Centre, get a *Time Out* at the newsstand. Take a two- or three-hour London bus tour. Have afternoon tea at Brown's or the Savoy. After a short rest, take an Original London Walk—Jack the Ripper Haunts, Ghosts of the West End (theater district), or Classic Murders and Crimes, stopping for a snack at one of the pubs on the tour.

Day 2: Start a little late today because of jet lag. Make your way to the British Museum with the exhibits Agatha helped unearth. Stroll through the St. John's Wood area along Northwick Terrace and the Regents Canal footpath. Have refreshment at Crockers Folly Pub. Take Jason's Trip on a canal boat from Little Venice to Camden Town and back, enjoying lunch aboard. Have dinner in the restaurant upstairs at the Sherlock Holmes. In the evening see *The Mousetrap*.

Day 3: Explore the elegant St. James/Mayfair Christie sites. Have a vegetarian (whole food) lunch at the Wren at St. James or a pub lunch at the Red Lion on Duke of York Street off Jermyn Street. See an exhibition at the Royal Academy of Arts, perhaps enjoying a little afternoon refreshment in the nice restaurant there before taking a turn through the Burlington Arcade. Dinner, then a concert.

Day 4: From Paddington Station take the train to Cholsey. Walk the quarter mile to St. Mary's Churchyard to visit Agatha Christie's grave. Taxi from the station into Wallingford. Visit the Castle Gardens, have a drink at the Regatta Hotel overlooking the Thames. Walk the Thames Footpath past Winterbrook House. Enjoy the typical English market town atmosphere. Walk back to Cholsey station. Return to London for dinner and theater. If you are going on to Oxford, take a taxi back to Cholsey Station. In Oxford, visit Max's colleges, All Souls and New College. Take tea at the Randolph. Return to London.

Day 5: Chelsea. Visit 22 Cresswell Place and 48 Swan Court. Tour the Royal Hospital and Ranelagh Gardens or the Chelsea Physic Garden. Enjoy the shops along Kings Road. Lunch at the Thames-side pub, King's Head and Eight Bells. Stroll along the Chelsea Embankment, noting the blue plaque houses. Cross the Thames to visit the Imperial War Museum. Dinner. Concert at Royal Festival Hall.

Day 6: Campden Hill for 47–48 Campden St. and 48 Sheffield Terrace. Walk through Holland Park. Visit the Leighton House Art Gallery and Museum. Spend the afternoon at some Christie-style shops, ending with tea at Liberty or Heals. Take in a play tonight, perhaps Shakespeare, the only author to outsell Christie, often alluded to in her works.

Day 7: Hampstead. End your week with the closest thing to a walk in the country. After seeing 22 Lawn Road Flats, stroll into Hampstead. Enjoy the High Street, picking up a map and guide to Hampstead at Waterstones Bookstore. Have a picnic lunch on the Heath. Visit John Keats' House. Enjoy the village atmosphere. Attend a concert at Kenwood House.

Alternative #1: For the ultimate Agatha Christie experience, take a day trip on the Orient Express into the English countryside, perhaps on Murder on the Orient Express; book the package, Haunts of Agatha Christie, which includes lodging at Brown's Hotel. Reservations required.

Alternative # 2: Early train to Harrogate. Visit the Old Swan Hotel, the Turkish Baths at the Assembly Rooms and the Royal Pump Room Museum. Walk in the Valley Gardens. After lunch at Betty's Cafe, take the train to York. Get a map in the visitor's center in the train station and walk into town. At the very least, visit the minster, explore the Shambles and walk as much of the city walls as time allows before the 2 hour and 10 minute train journey back into London.

Contacts and Resources for 7 Days in London

Day 1:

British Travel Centre, 1 Regent St. Walk-in callers only. Monday through Friday 9 a.m. to 6:30 p.m., Saturday until 5 p.m., Sunday 10 a.m. to 4 p.m. *Tube:* Piccadilly Circus.

The Original London Sightseeing Tour. Telephone: (0181) 877-1722. There are four separate Hop-on Hop-off Tours with joining points, many marked on London City bus signs.

Brown's Hotel, Albermarle and Dover St., Mayfair. Telephone: (0171) 493-6020. *Tube:* Green Park.

The Savoy Hotel, The Strand. Telephone: (0171) 836-4343. *Tube:* Charing Cross.

Original London Walks. Telephone: (0171) 624-3978. No

need to book in advance. Join at the designated Tube stop for the walk you choose.

Day 2:

The British Museum, Great Russell St. Telephone: (0171) 636-1555. Recorded Information: (0171) 580-1788. Monday through Saturday 10 a.m. to 5 p.m.; Sunday 2:30 p.m. to 6 p.m. (galleries must clear 10 minutes before closing) ; closed 3 days at Christmas, New Year's Day, Good Friday and bank holidays. *Tube:* Holborn, Tottenham Court Rd., Russell Square.

Crockers Folly Pub & Carvery, 24 Aberdeen Pl. Maida Vale, NW8. Telephone: (0171) 286-6608. *Tube:* Warwick Ave.

Jason's Trip, across from 60 Blomfield Road, Little Venice, W9. Telephone: (0171) 286-3428. To have tea or lunch, book in advance (0171) 286-6752. *Tube:* Warwick Ave.

Sherlock Holmes Pub & Restaurant (upstairs) 10 Northumberland St. WC1. Telephone: (0171) 930-2644. *Tube:* Charing Cross or Embankment.

St. Martin's Theatre, West St., WC2H 9NH. Telephone: (0171) 836-1443. *Tube:* Leicester Square.

Day 3:

Wren at St. James, 197 Piccadilly SW1. Telephone: (0171) 437-9419. *Tube:* Green Park or Piccadilly Circus.

Red Lion Pub, 2 Duke of York St. off Jermyn St., SW1. Telephone: (0171) 930-2030. *Tube:* Piccadilly Circus.

Royal Academy of Arts, Burlington House, Piccadilly W1.

Telephone: (0171) 439-7438. Daily 10 a.m. to 6 p.m. *Tube:* Piccadilly Circus or Green Park.

Burlington Arcade, Piccadilly. Telephone: (0171) 493-1764. Monday through Saturday 9 a.m. to 5:30 p.m. *Tube:* Bond St., Green Park or Piccadilly Circus.

Day 4:

Paddington Station, Praed St. Telephone: (0171) 262-6767. *Tube:* Paddington.

Wallingford Tourist Information Centre, 9 St. Martin's St. OX10 0AL. Telephone: (01491) 826-972. Fax: (01491) 826-550. Open Monday through Friday 9 a.m. to 1 p.m. & 2 p.m. to 5 pm.; closes Friday 4:30 p.m.

The George Hotel, High St. OX10 0BS. Telephone: (01491) 836-665. Fax: (01491) 825-593. Thistle Hotels: 1-800-847-4358.

The Regatta Hotel, Wallingford Bridge OX10 0BL. Telephone: (01491) 826-126.

The Cholsey & Wallingford Railway Preservation Society. Hithercroft Road. Telephone: (0491) 835-067. Limited operation so phone for schedule.

Oxford Tourist Information Centre, The Old School, Gloucester Green. Telephone: (01865) 726-871 Monday through Saturday 9:30 a.m. to 5 p.m.; Sunday 10 a.m. to 3:30 p.m.

The Randolph Hotel, Beaumont St., OX1 2LN. Telephone: (01865) 247-481.

New College, New College Lane, off Queen's Lane. Telephone: (01865) 279-555. Easter to September daily 11:30 a.m. to 5 p.m.; during term 2 p.m. to 5 p.m.

All Souls College, High Street at Cattle St. Telephone: (01865) 279-379. Monday through Friday 2 p.m. to 4:30 p.m.

Day 5:

Royal Hospital, Royal Hospital Road, Chelsea, SW3. Chapel and Museum open 10 a.m. to 12 noon, weekdays and 2 p.m. to 4 p.m. on Sundays (April through September for museum). Sundays: Holy Communion 8:30 a.m., Matins 11 a.m. after Governor's Parade at 10:40 a.m. when the pensioners wear their uniforms.

King's Head and Eight Bells, 50 Cheyne Walk, SW3. Telephone: (0171) 352-1820. *Tube:* Sloane Square.

Imperial War Museum, Lambeth Rd, SE1 6HZ. Telephone: (0171) 416-5000. Recorded information (0171) 820-1683. Daily 10 a.m. to 6 p.m.; closed three days at Christmas. *Tube:* Lambeth North or Elephant and Castle.

Royal Festival Hall at South Bank Centre, SE1. Telephone: (0171) 928-8800. Box Office 10 a.m. to 9 p.m. *Tube:* Waterloo or Embankment.

Day 6:

Leighton House Art Gallery and Museum, 12 Holland Park Road, Kensington. W14. Telephone: (0171) 602-3316. Monday through Saturday 11 a.m. to 5 p.m.; closed Sunday. *Tube:* Holland Park.

Libertys, 210–220 Regent St. Telephone: (0171) 734-1234. *Tube:* Oxford Circus.

Heals, 198 Tottenham Court Rd. Telephone: (0171) 636-1666. *Tube:* Goodge St.

Shakespeare's Globe Theater, Globe Walk, Bankside. Telephone: (0171) 401-9919. Performances May until mid-September only. Globe Museum, telephone: (0171) 928-6342. Open daily May through September 9 a.m. to 12:15 p.m. October through April 10 a.m. to 5 p.m. Closed December 24–5. *Tube:* London Bridge.

Royal Shakespeare Company, Barbicon Centre, Silk Street, EC21. Telephone: (0171) 638-8891.

Day 7:

Kenwood House, Hampstead Lane, Hampstead, NW3. Telephone: (0181) 348-1286. 10 a.m. to 6 p.m., til 4 p.m. October 1 through March 31, closed December 24–5. Saturday evening open air concerts, July through early September. Telephone: (0171) 413-1443. *Tube:* Highgate or Hampstead Heath.

Keats House, Keats Grove, NW3. Telephone: (0171) 435-2062. Monday through Friday 10 a.m. to 1 p.m., 2 p.m. to 6 p.m.; Saturday to 5 p.m.; Sunday, Easter and bank holidays 2 p.m. to 5 p.m. April to October; Monday through Friday 1 p.m. to 5 p.m.; Saturday 10 a.m. to 1 p.m.; 2 p.m. to 5 p.m.; Sunday 2 p.m. to 5 p.m. Closed 3 days at Christmas, New Year's Day, Good Friday, Easter Eve and May Day. *Tube:* Hampstead.

Alternative #1

Venice Simplon-Orient-Express Ltd., Sea Containers House, 20 Upper Ground, London SE1 9PF. Telephone: (0171) 928-6000. In the United States: 1-800-524-2420.

Alternative #2

Harrogate Tourist Information Centre, Royal Baths Assembly Rooms, Crescent Rd. Harrogate, HG1 2RR. Telephone: (01423) 537-357.

Betty's Cafe Tearoom, 1 Parliament St. Telephone: (01423) 569-861.

Turkish Sauna Suite, Royal Baths Assembly Rooms, Crescent Rd. Telephone: (01423) 562-498. Open seven days a week.

Pump Room Museum, Crown Place. Telephone: (01423) 503-340. Monday through Saturday 10 to 5, Sunday 2–5, April through October; November through March closes at 4.

Old Swan Hotel, Swan Road, Harrogate, HG1 2SR. Telephone: (01423) 500-055.

21-Day Itinerary

- 7 nights London

- 2 nights Harrogate

- 6 nights Torquay

- 2 nights Totnes

- 2 nights Wallingford

- 1 night Oxford

Day 1: Arrive in London. Visit the British Travel Centre, get a *Time Out* at the newsstand. Take a two- or three-hour London bus tour. Have afternoon tea at the Savoy. After a short rest, take an Original London Walk—Jack the Ripper Haunts, Ghosts of the West End (theater district), or Classic Murders and Crimes, getting a snack at one of the pubs on the tour.

Day 2: Start a little late today because of jet lag. Make your way to the British Museum to see the artifacts Agatha helped unearth. Stroll through the St. John's Wood area along Northwick Terrace and the Regents Canal footpath. Take Jason's Trip on a canal boat from Little Venice to Camden Town and back, having lunch aboard. Have dinner in the restaurant upstairs at the Sherlock Holmes. In the evening see *The Mousetrap*.

Day 3: Explore the elegant St. James/Mayfair Christie sites. Have a whole food (vegetarian) lunch at the Wren at St.

James or a pub lunch at the Red Lion on Duke of York Street off Jermyn Street. See an exhibition at the Royal Academy of Arts, perhaps enjoying a little afternoon refreshment in the nice restaurant there before taking a turn through the Burlington Arcade. Dinner, then a concert.

Day 4: Shop in the Christie manner. Don't miss the Army and Navy Stores, Heals, Libertys, Lillywhites and any others your energy allows. Treat yourself to lunch in one of the department store restaurants. Take in a noontime concert at St. Martin-in-the-Fields off Trafalgar Square. Be sure to end the shopping expedition with chocolates from Charbonnel et Walker. Compare Flemings and Brown's to judge for yourself which is the model for Bertram's in *At Bertram's Hotel.* Take tea at Brown's. Theater in the evening.

Day 5: Chelsea. Visit 22 Cresswell Place and 48 Swan Court. Tour the Royal Hospital and Ranelagh Gardens. Enjoy the shops along the Kings Road. Lunch at the Thames-side pub, King's Head and Eight Bells. Stroll along the Chelsea Embankment, noting the blue plaque houses. Cross the Thames to visit the Imperial War Museum. Dinner. Concert at Royal Festival Hall.

Day 6: Campden Hill for 47–48 Campden St. and 48 Sheffield Terrace. Enjoy a retreat in Holland Park and the Leighton House Art Gallery and Museum. Try a little celebrity spotting during lunch or dinner at the Room at the Halcyon Hotel in Holland Park. Visit the Victoria and Albert Museum or the Tate Art Gallery. Take in an evening performance at Holland House or a Shakespeare play.

Day 7: Hampstead. End your week with the closest thing to a walk in the country. After seeing 22 Lawn Road Flats, stroll into Hampstead. Enjoy the High Street, picking up a map and guide to Hampstead at Waterstones Bookstore. Have a picnic lunch on the Heath. Visit John Keats' House. Enjoy the village atmosphere. Attend a concert at Kenwood House. Prepare to leave London tomorrow.

Day 8: Break the train journey to Harrogate at York. Check your bags at the station. Get a map at the visitor's center there and walk into town. Visit the minster, explore the Shambles, walk the city walls. After tea, collect your bags and resume your journey to Harrogate, arriving in time for dinner. Two nights in Harrogate.

Day 9: Visit the Old Swan Hotel, the Turkish Baths at the Assembly Rooms and the Royal Pump Room Museum. Have lunch or afternoon tea at Betty's Cafe. Shop. Walk through the Stray and the Valley Gardens. Dinner, perhaps in the Agatha Christie Room at the Old Swan.

Day 10: Train journey to Torquay for late afternoon arrival. Stop at the Tourist Information Centre to gather material. Check into hotel.

Day 11: Walk the first half of the Agatha Christie Mile, beginning with Kents Caverns and the Torquay Museum and ending with tea on the terrace at the Imperial Hotel.

Day 12: Walk the other half of the Agatha Christie Mile, beginning at the Pavilion, visiting Torre Abbey and the Grand Hotel. Visit Cockington Village.

Day 13: Take the train to Totnes. If this isn't a Tuesday, try to make Day 16 or 17 a Tuesday to see the townspeople in their Elizabethan costumes. Join the Dart River cruise past Greenway House and visit Dartmouth. Ferry across to Kingswear and take the stream train back to Paignton. Train or taxi to Torquay for the night.

Day 14: Revisit some of the scenes of Christie's childhood at All Saints Church in Tor Mohun. Train to Churston to see the Agatha Christie stained glass.

Day 15: Train to Newton Abbot. Taxi to Haytor Vale. Walk out on Dartmoor to Hay Tor and picnic on the moor. Tea at the Moorland Hotel in the Agatha Christie Lounge. Return to Torquay for the night.

Day 16: Train to Totnes. Taxi to Bigbury on Sea for Burgh Island. Lunch at the Burgh Island Hotel (reservations required) with a stroll around the island before or after lunch. Refreshment at the Pilchard Inn. Return to Totnes for the night.

Day 17: Public transportation to Salcombe or hire a driver for the day. Explore the harbor and walk the route described in *Towards Zero*. Picnic on the beach. Return to Totnes for the night.

Day 18: Train journey for afternoon arrival at Cholsey. Walk out to St. Mary's Churchyard to visit the Christie/Mallowan grave. Taxi to Wallingford. Overnight in Wallingford.

Day 19: Collect materials from the Tourist Information Centre. Walk the Thames Footpath that passes below Winterbrook House. Visit the Castle Gardens, have a drink at the Regatta Hotel overlooking the Thames. Enjoy the typical English market town atmosphere, especially if this is a Friday, market day. Overnight in Wallingford.

Day 20: Fifteen-minute train ride to Oxford. Check into your hotel for your last night. Visit Max's colleges—All Souls and New College. Wander at your leisure in the city of dreaming spires. Take tea at the Randolph.

Day 21: Bus to Heathrow or Gatwick for the journey home.

Contacts and Resources for a 21-Day Stay

Whenever visiting a town or city, go to the Tourist Information Centre as soon as possible for help in getting oriented. Most staff members are volunteers, love their area and enjoy talking about it.

Day 1:

British Travel Centre, 1 Regent St. Walk-in callers only. Monday through Friday 9 a.m. to 6:30 p.m.; Saturday until 5 p.m.; Sunday 10 a.m. to 4 p.m. *Tube:* Piccadilly Circus.

The Original London Sightseeing Tour. Telephone: (0181) 877-1722. There are four separate Hop-on Hop-off Tours with joining points, many marked on London City bus signs.

The Savoy Hotel, The Strand. Telephone: (0171) 836-4343. *Tube:* Charing Cross.

Original London Walks. Telephone: (0171) 624-3978. No need to book in advance. Join at the designated Tube stop for your chosen tour.

Day 2:

The British Museum, Great Russell St. Telephone: (0171) 636-1555. Recorded Information: (0171) 580-1788. Monday through Saturday 10 a.m. to 5 p.m.; Sunday 2:30 p.m. to 6 p.m. (galleries cleared 10 minutes before closing) ; closed 3 days at Christmas, New Year's Day, Good Friday and bank holidays. *Tube:* Holborn, Tottenham Court Rd., Russell Square.

Crockers Folly Pub & Carvery, 24 Aberdeen Pl. Maida Vale, NW8. Telephone: (0171) 286-6608. *Tube:* Warwick Ave.

Jason's Trip, across from 60 Blomfield Road, Little Venice, W9. Telephone: (0171) 286-3428. To have lunch on board, book in advance (0171) 286-6752. *Tube:* Warwick Ave.

Sherlock Holmes Pub & Restaurant (upstairs), 10 Northumberland St. WC1. Telephone: (0171) 930-2644. *Tube:* Charing Cross or Embankment.

St. Martin's Theatre, West St., WC2H 9NH. Telephone: (0171) 836-1443. *Tube:* Leicester Square.

Day 3:

Wren at St. James, 197 Piccadilly SW1. Telephone: (0171) 437-9419. *Tube:* Green Park or Piccadilly Circus.

Red Lion Pub, 2 Duke of York St. off Jermyn St., SW1. Telephone: (0171) 930-2030. *Tube:* Piccadilly Circus.

Royal Academy of Arts, Burlington House, Piccadilly W1. Telephone: (0171) 439-7438. Daily 10 a.m. to 6 p.m. *Tube:* Piccadilly Circus or Green Park.

Burlington Arcade, Piccadilly. Telephone: (0171) 493-1764. Monday through Saturday 9 a.m. to 5:30 p.m. *Tube:* Bond St., Green Park or Piccadilly Circus.

Day 4:

General Shopping Hours in London: Monday through Saturday 9 a.m./10 a.m. to 5:30 p.m./6 p.m.; some shops open for late shopping Wednesday or Thursday until 8 p.m. A few of the largest have some Sunday hours.

Army and Navy Stores, 101–105 Victoria St. Telephone: (0171) 834-1234. *Tube:* Victoria

Heals, 198 Tottenham Court Rd. Telephone: (0171) 636-1666. *Tube:* Goodge St.

Liberty, 210–220 Regent St. Telephone: (0171) 734-1234. Monday, Tuesday, Friday, Saturday 9:30 a.m. to 6 p.m.; Wednesday 10 a.m. to 6 p.m.; Thursday 9:30 a.m. to 7:30 p.m. *Tube:* Oxford Circus.

Lillywhites Ltd. 24–36 Lower Regent St., Piccadilly. Telephone: (0171) 915-4000. Monday, Wednesday, Friday 9:30 a.m. to 5:30 p.m.; Thursday 9:30 a.m. to 7 p.m.; Saturday 9:30 a.m. to 6 p.m. *Tube:* Piccadilly Circus.

St. Martin-in-the-Fields, Trafalgar Square. Telephone: (0171) 839 1930. Concerts Monday, Tuesday, Friday at 1 p.m. and evenings. *Tube:* Trafalgar Square.

Charbonnel et Walker (in the Burlington Arcade), 1 Royal Arcade, 28 Old Bond St. Telephone: (0171) 491 0939. Monday through Friday 9:30 a.m. to 5 p.m.; Saturday 10 a.m. to 5 p.m. *Tube:* Bond St. Green Park or Piccadilly Circus.

Flemings Hotel and Luxury Apartments, 7–12 Half Moon St., Mayfair. Telephone: (0171) 499-2964 or 1-800-348-4685. *Tube:* Green Park.

Brown's Hotel, Albermarle and Dover St., Mayfair. Telephone: (0171) 493-6020. *Tube:* Green Park.

Day 5:

Royal Hospital, Royal Hospital Road, Chelsea, SW3. Chapel and Museum open 10 a.m. to noon, weekdays and 2 p.m. to 4 p.m. on Sundays (April through September for museum). Sundays: Holy Communion 8:30 a.m., Matins 11 a.m. after Governor's Parade at 10:40 a.m. when the pensioners wear their red (in summer) or blue (in winter) uniforms. *Tube:* Sloane Square.

King's Head and Eight Bells, 50 Cheyne Walk, SW3. Telephone: (0171) 352-1820. *Tube:* Sloane Square.

Imperial War Museum, Lambeth Rd SE1 6HZ. Telephone: (0171) 416-5000. Recorded information (0171) 820-1683. Daily 10 a.m. to 6 p.m.; closed 3 p.m. at Christmas. *Tube:* Lambeth North or Elephant and Castle.

Royal Festival Hall at South Bank Centre, SE1. Telephone: (0171) 928-8800. Box Office 10 a.m. to 9 p.m. *Tube:* Waterloo or Embankment.

Day 6:

Leighton House Art Gallery and Museum, 12 Holland Park Road, Kensington W14. Telephone: (0171) 602-3316. Monday through Saturday 11 a.m. to 5 p.m.; closed Sunday. *Tube:* Holland Park.

The Room at the Halcyon in the Halcyon Hotel, 81 Holland Park Ave. Telephone: (0171) 221-5411. Monday through Thursday noon to 2:30 p.m. and 7 p.m. to 10:30 p.m.; Friday noon to 2:30 p.m.; Friday and Saturday 7 p.m. to 11 p.m.; Sunday noon to 3 p.m. and 7 p.m. to 10 p.m. *Tube:* Holland Park.

Victoria and Albert Museum, Cromwell Rd., SW7. Telephone: (0171) 938-8500. Monday noon to 5 p.m., Tuesday through Sunday 10 a.m. to 5:50 p.m. Jazz Brunch Sunday 11 a.m. to 3 p.m. *Tube:* South Kensington.

Tate Gallery. Beside the Thames on Millbank, SW1. Telephone: (0171) 887-8000. Monday through Saturday 10 a.m. to 5:50 p.m.; Sunday 2 p.m. to 5:50 p.m. *Tube:* Pimlico.

Holland House—Holland Park Theatre. Telephone: (0171) 602-7856. Open air music, dance, theatre performances, mid-June to late August at 7:30 p.m. Telephone: (0171) 603-1123 for information. *Tube:* Kensington High Street.

Shakespeare's Globe Theater, Globe Walk, Bankside. Telephone: (0171) 401-9919. Performances May until mid-September only. Globe Museum, telephone: (0171) 928-6342. Open daily May through September 9 a.m. to 12:15 p.m. October through April 10 a.m. to 5 p.m. Closed December 24–5. *Tube:* London Bridge.

Royal Shakespeare Company, Barbicon Centre, Silk Street EC21. Telephone: (0171) 638-8891. *Tube:* Barbicon.

Open Air Theatre, Inner Circle, Regent's Park NW1. Telephone: (0171) 486-2431/1933. Summer only. *Tube:* Baker Street or Regent's Park.

Day 7:

Keats House, Keats Grove, NW3. Telephone: (0171) 435-2062. April through October, Monday through Friday 10 a.m. to 1 p.m., 2 p.m. to 6 p.m.; Saturday 10 a.m. to 1 p.m., 2 p.m. to 5 p.m.; Sunday, Easter and bank holidays 2 p.m. to 5 p.m. April to October; Monday through Friday 1 p.m. to 5 p.m.; Saturday 10 a.m. to 1 p.m., 2 p.m. to 5 p.m.; Sunday 2 p.m. to 5 p.m. Closed 3 days at Christmas, New Year's Day, Good Friday, Easter Eve and May Day. November through March: same hours but Monday through Friday closes one hour earlier. *Tube:* Belsize Park or Hampstead.

Kenwood House, Hampstead Lane, Hampstead, NW3. Telephone: (0181) 348-1286. 10 a.m. to 6 p.m., but only until 4 p.m. October 1 through March 31, closed December 24–5. Open air concerts July though early September. Telephone: (0171) 413-1443. *Tube:* Highgate or Hampstead Heath.

Day 8:

Kings Cross Station, Euston Rd. Telephone: (0171) 278-2477.

York Tourist Information Centre, DeGrey Rooms, Exhibition Square. Telephone: (01904) 621-756.

York Tourism Bureau, 20 George Hudson St. Telephone: (01904) 554-455. Fax: (01904) 554-460.

Day 9:

Harrogate Tourist Information Centre, Royal Baths Assembly Rooms, Crescent Rd. Harrogate, HG1 2RR. Telephone: (01423) 537-357.

Betty's Cafe Tearoom, 1 Parliament St. Telephone: (01423) 569-861.

Turkish Sauna Suite, Royal Baths Assembly Rooms, Crescent Rd. Telephone: (01423) 562-498. Open 7 days a week.

Pump Room Museum, Crown Place (01423) 503-340. Monday through Saturday 10 a.m. to 5 p.m., Sunday 2 p.m. to 5 p.m., April through October; November through March closes at 4 p.m.

Old Swan Hotel, Swan Road, Harrogate, HG1 2SR. Telephone: (01423) 500-055.

Day 10:

The English Riviera Tourist Board, The Tourist Centre, Vaughan Parade, Torquay TQ2 5JG. Telephone: (01803) 297-428; Fax: (01803) 214-885.

The Imperial Hotel, Park Hill Rd., Torquay TQ1 2DG. Telephone: (01803) 294-301 or 1-800-225-5843.

The Grand Hotel, Torbay Rd., Torquay TQ2 6NT. Telephone: (01803) 296-677.

Osborne Hotel, Hesketh Crescent, Torquay TQ1 2LL. Telephone: (01803) 213-311.

Day 11:

Torquay Museum, 529 Babbacombe Rd., Torquay TQ1 1HG.

Telephone: (01803) 293-975. Open Easter through October, Monday through Saturday 10 a.m. to 4:45 p.m.; Sunday 1:30 p.m. to 4:45 p.m.; November to Easter, Monday through Friday 10 a.m. to 4:45 p.m.

Kents Cavern, Ilsham Rd., Torquay TQ1 2JF. Telephone: (01803) 294-059. Open daily 10 a.m. to 5 p.m./9 p.m., depending on season.

The Imperial Hotel, Park Hill Rd., Torquay TQ1 2DG. Telephone: (01803) 294-301 or 1-800-225-5843.

Day 12:

Torre Abbey, The Kings Drive, Torquay TQ2 5JX. Telephone: (01803) 293-593. Open April through October daily 9:30 a.m. to 6 p.m.; November through March: parties only by appointment.

Cockington Country Park, Torquay TQ2 6XA. Telephone: (01803) 690-495.

The Grand Hotel, Torbay Rd. Torquay TQ2 6NT. Telephone: (01803) 296-677.

Day 13:

Dart Pleasure Craft, River Link. Telephone: (01803) 834-488.

Dartmouth Tourist Information Centre, The Engine House, Mayor's Avenue, Dartmouth TQ6 9YY. Telephone: (01803) 834-224.

Torbay and Dartmouth Steam Railway, Queens Park Station, Paignton TQ4 6AF. Telephone: (01803) 555-872.

Open Easter, then end of May to early October 10 a.m. to 4 p.m. daily. Santa Specials in December.

Day 14:

All Saints Torre, Bampfylde Road, Torquay. All Saints Vicarage, 45 Barton Rd., Torquay TQ1 4DT. Telephone: (01803) 326-692. Mass daily. Sunday evensong.

Day 15:

Newton Abbot Tourist Information Centre.

Moorland Hotel, Haytor, Dartmoor, Newton Abbot TQ13 9XT. Telephone: (01364) 661-407.

Day 16:

Totnes Tourist Information Centre, The Plains, Totnes TQ9 5EJ. Telephone: (01803) 863-168.

Burgh Island Hotel, Bigbury-on-Sea, South Devon TQ7 4BG. Telephone: (01548) 810-514.

Day 17:

Salcombe Tourist Information Centre, Council Hall, Market St., Salcombe TQ8 8DE. Telephone: (01548) 843-927.

Days 18 and 19:

Wallingford Tourist Information Centre, 9 St. Martin's St. OX10 0AL. Telephone: (01491) 826-972 Fax: (01491) 826-550. Open Monday through Friday 9 a.m. to 1 p.m. & 2 p.m. to 5 p.m.; closes Friday 4:30 p.m.

The George Hotel, High St. OX10 0BS. Telephone: (01491) 836-665 Fax: (01491) 825-593. Thistle Hotels: 1-800-847-4358.

The Regatta Hotel, Wallingford Bridge OX10 0BL. Telephone: (01491) 826-126.

The Cholsey & Wallingford Railway Preservation Society. Hithercroft Road. Telephone: (0491) 835-067. Limited operation so phone for schedule.

Day 20:

Oxford Tourist Information Centre, The Old School, Gloucester Green. Telephone: (01865) 726-871 Monday through Saturday 9:30 a.m. to 5 p.m.; Sunday 10 a.m. to 3:30 p.m.

The Randolph Hotel, Beaumont St., OX1 2LN. Telephone: (01865) 247-481. Forte Hotel Chain 1-800-225-5843.

New College, New College Lane, off Queen's Lane. Telephone: (01865) 279-555. Easter to September daily 11:30 a.m. to 5 p.m.; during term 2 p.m. to 5 p.m.

All Souls College, High Street at Cattle St. Telephone: (01865) 279-379. Monday through Friday 2 p.m. to 4:30 p.m.

Tried and True in Oxford, No Christie Connection

Eastgate Hotel, 23 Merton St., The High, OX1 4BE. Telephone: (01865) 248-244. Also part of the Forte Chain: 1-800-225-5843. The bus to Heathrow stops on the High, just steps from the hotel. If you're an Inspector Morse fan, you'll enjoy knowing that the cast often stays here when filming.

Index

Judith Diana Hurdle, a writer and avid mystery fan, has traveled extensively in England and lived there for an extended period. With grants from the National Endowment for the Humanities, the DeWitt Wallace Foundation, the Council for Basic Education and the Eli Lilly Foundation, she has conducted research there on the British Raj and on English writers Charles Dickens, Anthony Powell and C. P. Snow. Hurdle is a member of the British Society of Women Writers and Journalists and lives in Valparaiso, Indiana, where she teaches English. This is her first book.

I Should Have
Stayed Home
The Worst Trips of Great Writers

Edited by
ROGER RAPOPORT *and*
MARGUERITA CASTANERA

In this national bestseller,
50 top travel writers,
novelists, and journalists
including **Isabel Allende,
Jan Morris, Barbara
Kingsolver, Paul Theroux,
Mary Morris, Dominique
Lapierre, Pico Iyer, Eric
Hansen, Rick Steves, Tony
Wheeler,** and **Mary
Mackey** tell the stories
of their greatest travel
disasters. From the electric
baths of Tokyo to the
Night of the Army Ants in
Guatemala, this unforget-
table book will make you
unfasten your seatbelt for
the belly laugh of the travel
season. Guaranteed to
whet your appetite or
make you cancel your
reservations.

ISBN: 1-57143-014-8

$15.95
TRADE PAPERBACK
256 PAGES

*One of "the five best travel
books of the year. Feisty, funny,
a bracing alternative to the
Technicolor-sunset school of
travel writing."*
—San Francisco Examiner

I've Been Gone
Far Too Long

Scientists' Worst Trips

Edited by MONIQUE
BORGERHOFF-MULDER *and*
WENDY LOGSDON

In this hilarious anthology,
26 research scientists go off
the deep ends of the earth.
Travel with a young
researcher in Dian Fossey's
camp as she is handed a
gun and told to go out and
shoot a gorilla poacher. See
how a scientist reacts
when he discovers a
poisonous bushmaster in
his bidet. From bush pilots
and endangered species to
Land Rover nightmares,
this hair-raising book will
keep you up past dawn.
This book is a tribute to
the courage of an intrepid
band of researchers who
have risked all to bring
home the truth. Authors
are contributing their
royalties to the Wildlife
Conservation Society.

ISBN: 1-57143-054-7

$15.95
TRADE PAPERBACK
296 PAGES

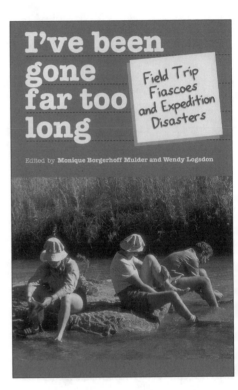

"*People in khaki and pith
helmets can be funny.
Some could start second
careers as comedians should
they be denied tenure.*"
—American Library
Association Booklist

After the Death of a Salesman

Business Trips to Hell

By ROGER RAPOPORT

In this sequel to bestselling *I Should Have Stayed Home* and *I've Been Gone Far Too Long,* business people tell of their greatest travel disasters—from the emergency room to the paddy wagon. Read this book and you'll be happy you weren't traveling with: oilman Jack Howard, cruise scout Marcia Wick, engineer Joe Carr, conductor Murray Gross, bookseller Monica Holmes, investor Jack Branagh, sales rep Teri Goldsmith, or publisher Cynthia Frank. Dedicated to the memory of Willie Loman, this tribute to corporate road warriors includes an inside and affectionate look at the book publishing business and offers an amusing view of everything they don't want to know in business school.

ISBN: 1-57143-062-8

$15.95
TRADE PAPERBACK
224 PAGES

"If you're interested in finding out just what it's like for the men and women of the road, this book offers a terrifically funny and occasionally touching insight"

—American Library Association Booklist

I'll Never Get Lost Again
The Complete Guide to Improving Your Sense of Direction

By LINDA GREKIN

Millions of people including Ann Landers, Joan Baez, Beverly Sills and Dr. Kenneth Blanchard have a poor sense of direction. In this groundbreaking book, Linda Grekin explains why some people never get from point A to point B and what, if anything, they can do about it. Based on original research, talks with top scientific experts and hundreds of interviews with the directionally challenged, this book offers a provocative and lively examination of the seventh sense—the sense of direction. Grekin shows why millions of otherwise competent people, from children to CEOs, become easily disoriented and are often unable to find their way. Written with wit and wisdom, *I'll Never Get Lost Again* is the perfect traveling companion

ISBN: 1-57143-069-5

$12.95
TRADE PAPERBACK
128 PAGES

"I'll Never Get Lost Again *will bring comfort to many."*
—Dallas Morning News

THE GETAWAY GUIDES

Each of these guides is an ideal itinerary planner for short or long trips. Organized with daily trip schedules, each book gently guides you to well-known and off-the-beaten-track destinations with helpful directions, recommended schedules, and convenient lodging and dining recommendations. Written by experts who visit every one of the places they recommend, the Getaway Guides can be used for long weekends, week-long trips, or grand three week tours. Perfect for budget travelers and those who prefer luxury, each Getaway Guide is years in the making to insure that your trip is a winner from beginning to end. Selective and fun to read, each book reveals the secrets travel writers usually reserve for their closest friends.

The Getaway Guide to California

By Roger Rapoport

ISBN 1-57143-068-7. $15.95. Available June 1999.

The Getaway Guide to the American Southwest

By Richard Harris

ISBN 1-57143-073-3. $15.95. Available July 1999.

The Getaway Guide to Colorado

By Roger Rapoport

ISBN 1-57143-072-5. $15.95. Available July 1999.

Our books are available at your local bookstore, or contact RDR Books at 4456 Piedmont Avenue, Oakland, CA 94611. Phone (510) 595-0595. Fax (510) 595-0598. Email: rdrbooks@lanminds.com.

See our books on the Web at http://www.rdrbooks.com.

9/00

GAYLORD S